Fiona Armstrong's

COMMUTER'S COOKBOOK

Fiona Armstrong's

COMMUTER'S
COOKBOOK

Arrive Home Late — Dine On Time!

Neil Wilson Publishing • Glasgow

Published by Neil Wilson Publishing Ltd
303a The Pentagon Centre
36 Washington Street
GLASGOW
G3 8AZ
Tel: 0141-221-1117
Fax: 0141-221-5363

A catalogue record for this book is available from the British Library
ISBN 1-897784-40-6

Dedication
To my wonderful parents, Pauline and Bob, for helping me test all the food.
To Rod, my husband, for eating it.

Useful books and other sources.
All of Delia Smith's books!
Real Fast Food, Nigel Slater
Ten Minute Cuisine, Pierre Moine and Henrietta Green
The Guinness Book of Records
Thanks also to the Department of Transport and Richard Foster in their
Research Department who let me delve into their library.

Consultant editor: Derek A. Kingwell
Illustrations by Doreen Shaw

Typeset in 11.5/12pt Helvetica by The Write Stuff, Glasgow
Tel: 0141-339-8279. E-mail: *wilson_i@cqm.co.uk*

Printed by Scotprint Ltd, Musselburgh

Contents

On the Way...   49

Introduction

To travel hopefully is a better thing than to arrive and
the true success is to labour...

Robert Louis Stevenson (El Dorado)

I'm certain that RLS did not have the modern-day commuter in mind when he penned this, but words like 'travelling hopefully' and 'labouring' will certainly ring a few bells for most of us! One thing is sure: being a commuter can be hell and there are thousands who agree. Anyone who has ever had to travel to work is bound to have his or her own horror story to report.

Mine is a tale of arriving home 17 hours late one winter's weekend after a mix of trains, cars and coaches failed to come up to scratch. Mind you, I was lucky, for some people never get there at all!

I've been travelling in one way or another since I was two months old. Then, my father worked in West Africa with the Colonial Service and we regularly crossed continents by a variety of trains, boats and planes. Some trips were more memorable than others — like the one across Nigeria in 1962. It began badly when we got off the boat at Lagos and headed for customs. As we declared the few luxury goods we were bringing in, the officer suddenly announced that he would have to tax us, not on my mother's coffee-maker or brandy, but on three small bicycles.

'Tax the bikes?' she queried. 'But they're just toys for the little ones!'

'Madam, these are not toys,' was the stern reply. 'These are means of transport for the children to get to work!'

We were at the time, four, six and seven years old. To solve the problem, my mother told us all to cry loudly. The customs officer got fed up and let us go.

As we headed towards our train, my mother found, to our

childish amusement and to her horror, that the carriage we had reserved, had not only been double-booked, but quadruple-booked for different groups of people, all clamouring loudly for the privilege of a seat on the 36-hour, 600-mile trek north. As we were the largest family with three children, three bikes and a mother, we won the toss, and so began my longest train journey ever.

It was long, it was airless and it was hot. True, the windows did open, but the engine never got up enough speed to allow a welcoming draught to filter into the carriage. In fact, at one stage, we were going so slowly that local traders were able to walk alongside keeping pace, as they noisily tried to press African carvings to us through the window, hopefully for a little cash, or at the very least, bottles of lemonade.

And thank God for the lemonade! There wasn't a drop of water to be had anywhere. So not only did we drink the lemonade, we used it to brush our teeth, wash our hands and mop our brows.

As far as food went, it was definitely not varied. For breakfast we were offered tinned mixed vegetables; for lunch, the steward came round with tinned mixed vegetables and for dinner — yes, once again it was tins of mixed vegetables.

We can laugh about it now, but I suppose that travel like this was a good preparation for later life because it was 20 years later that I found myself as a Thames Valley commuter, working in Reading and living in London.

My job was as a journalist with a local radio station and, in an area packed with commuting folk, one of the most important services we offered was the essential early-morning summary of train and traffic advice. One morning I nearly caused domestic pandemonium in Reading when I kept informing the good folk that it was eight o'clock in the morning, when it was, in fact, only seven o'clock.

As well as time-keeping for our audience, I was regularly sent out to cover stories about commuter journeys to and from hell. It wasn't quite a case of constantly washing in lemonade and eating canned vegetables, but that run along the M4 into London presented its own special problems.

I remember interviewing one man who recounted how he had been making the trip into London for 25 years when he finally broke down, and when I say that, I don't mean the car. He told me how he finally snapped one morning when he encountered his fifth set of traffic cones. As he joined yet another motorway queue, he got out of the car and sat down and wept on the hard shoulder. I do hope that he eventually gave up commuting since I should hate to think he was still going through the same pain.

But it didn't seem to affect Ralph Ransome of Kent, who notched up more than a million miles of unrelenting commuting in his lifetime! As one of British Rail's best customers, for 73 years he regularly caught the early service from Birchampton to London to get to work in the city. He eventually retired at the age of 93, having clocked up the equivalent of travelling 39 times around the world and was rewarded for his perseverance with a watch and ride in the driver's cab.

I was not, (fortunately I think), destined to follow in Mr Ransome's footsteps as a daily commuter. What I did do, though, was to get a newscasting job at ITN in London, and then marry a Scotsman. In short I became a long-distance commuter.

I worked it out that it was 325 miles from our home on the Border to the centre of London. I suppose by commuting standards that's quite a distance, but it's all relative because I now work with a colleague at the BBC who commutes each week from London to New York!

However, the trip from home to work took me a good five hours by road and so it was the train that began to take the strain (or should I say, make the strain?!). And thus began my years of long-distance commuting. Down to London at the start of the working week, back again at the weekend. I suppose it just became a way of life, although I have never done it as effortlessly as one of my fellow newscasters.

He was the late Leonard Parkin and the hugely popular presenter on the lunchtime ITN news. Each weekday, between 1.00 and 1.30pm, he would deliver the events of the day in his characteristically charming and authoritative style. But when Friday arrived — if you watched him closely — his 'goodbye' could often be accompanied by half a wink which was the secret signal to the folks up in Yorkshire that he was heading north for the weekend, and they should get his cottage ready.

But signs apart, I reckon that over the past eight years I have spent a good ten hours a week on trains and that equates to more than 20 days spent on trains every year! Twenty full days — what do you do with all that time? I've heard of some commuters who write novels and plays, while others form study clubs to improve themselves. I used to write a lot and have kept diaries of my journeys north and south. Some of these are best forgotten, like the late trains, the dirty trains and the rowdy trains...but others are really memorable.

Such as the time I returned from the restaurant car to find that my luggage was missing. No, it hadn't been stolen, but it had been thrown off the train at Lancaster because the guard thought it contained a bomb! Presumably, my alarm clock had been ticking away loudly inside. Still, better safe than sorry! Or when the keys to the galley of the restaurant car were accidentally left at Euston Station. There we were, weary travellers all expecting refreshments on our long journey north and about to be disappointed when the kitchen staff took an bold step and broke into the galley with what appeared to be a machete.

Then there's the memory of a Christmas Eve when we chugged along with a failing engine through the wintry Lake District with the onboard lights and heating failing and our spirits dropping by the mile. I, for one, had gloomy visions of a not-so-festive season on top of Shap summit, but the cheery catering crew gave out hot drinks and sang carols and we did make it home for Christmas, albeit several hours late.

Or the time I put my back out. I'd been fishing earlier that day and must have overdone it on the casting. By the time we got to Crewe I was in a sorry state, and as the train pulled into Euston I was bent double. The guard, thinking that I was a hospital case, guided me out to a cab, tut-tutting at the thought of anyone letting me get on the train in that condition. The cab driver called me 'Missus' until I lifted up my pain-stricken face.

'You're never that girl on the telly, are you?! Go on, tell us the news is you've got a bad back!'

Weakly, I begged him to take me to the nearest pharmacy to get some painkillers...

The other thing I used to do on the train was plan the week's meals. I'm married to a man who likes his food, and being a Borderer, he likes me to cook it for him. Since I love cooking, it's something I don't argue about.

On the train, I would do the cooking in my head — that was the easy bit, preparing the menus mentally. It was just putting it all into practice when I got off at the other end, tired and jaded, which was more difficult. Also, I don't need to tell you that a life of work and travel leaves precious little time for essential things like shopping. The commuting cook, I decided, would have to be quick, organised and resourceful.

So, I've gathered together some of the recipes I've used over the years. They are either quick to prepare and cook, or they can be prepared in advance, or they are recipes to make out of nothing — and by that, I mean a quick meal to rustle up simply by using a few basic storecupboard items.

A few are original, but most are probably not. If I know whose recipes they are, I have said so. If I have stolen anyone's recipe and not credited them, I apologise. I must also say here that although all the recipes have been tested, tastes do differ, so feel free to add less salt, more lemon, etc...

Yes, it is hard being a commuter — but a weary traveller does not have to be a weary cook. So, here goes, all aboard for The *Commuter's Cookbook!*

Fiona Armstrong
June 1995

Preparing to Go...

...COMMUTING IS THE MAIN REASON WHY PEOPLE TRAVEL IN BRITAIN. THE SECOND REASON IS SHOPPING. THE AVERAGE PERSON COMMUTES JUST UNDER 1200 MILES A YEAR. ADULT LONDON MALES SPEND AN AVERAGE 92 MINUTES PER WEEKDAY TRAVELLING. THE AVERAGE FOR A WOMAN IS 71 MINUTES.

Well, there you have it, we're a nation of travellers and rushers. But it doesn't matter how much of a rush you're in, or how hellish the rush hour was — we've got to eat and with a bit of luck, eat well.

I hope that the following will help you along the way to a quick, easy and delicious time in the kitchen. That's the good news. The bad news, I'm afraid, is that you can't produce something out of nothing. So forget about magic. Everything requires some effort, if only the movement of reaching for the tin opener, or dissolving a stock cube. But life for the commuting cook can be made a little less fraught by being organised.

Planning ahead really helps. For example, soaking dried beans the night before you need them, or preparing vegetables in advance, or taking out frozen foods to defrost whilst you're at work. So try to think ahead a little. I'm a great one for lists, but you may be happier without them.

It also helps to **make extra portions** of things you like to eat. Most of it can be frozen or stored and used at a later date. For example, chopped parsley keeps well in the freezer and breadcrumbs won't come to any harm for a week or so in an airtight jar. If you're cooking chilli, make a bit more and freeze some to use later in the month. A friend of mine always makes two omelettes when she cooks with eggs. One to eat there and then and the other to eat cold the following day, sliced into a salad with a herby French dressing and some crusty bread.

Read recipes through to the end to make sure you have

everything you need. There's nothing worse than starting to cook and discovering that you are missing one vital ingredient! Or getting halfway through and finding out that the sauce you are making has to stand for 2 hours before proceeding with the rest of the recipe...

When cooking, it really does help to **gather everything together** before you start work. Grate the cheese, squeeze the lemon and measure the flour.

Where possible, **make things in advance**. You've got fridges and freezers, so use them ...

One of the most important things for the commuting cook is the **store-cupboard**. We've all cluttered up the kitchen (I probably still do) with all manner of inconvenient 'convenience' foods that are still there a year later. What you need are the basics like flour, salt and sugar, and here are a few of the other ingredients I always like to have in stock.

TINNED FOOD

Tinned tomatoes are a must. Buy them ready-chopped, with or without herbs and garlic, and you've got the base for a tomato soup, a bean casserole or a spaghetti bolognaise.

Tinned beans are useful for salads and soups and especially for vegetarian dishes. Canned haricots or butter beans are delicious served in a tasty white sauce and chick peas make a lovely hummous, whizzed in the food processor with garlic, oil and lemon juice.

Tinned soup can double as a cook-in sauce for chicken, but ensure that you buy good quality product; it really does make a difference.

Tinned fish is the commuting cook's good friend. Tuna is great in a salad, or with pasta, and tinned salmon makes a quick pâté. Tinned sardines in olive oil are useful for a quick snack on toast. Anchovy fillets are wonderful for pepping up a pasta, dressing a pizza or adding bite to scrambled egg.

Tinned fruit, such as tinned cherries are good for puddings or for a cherry sauce with ice-cream. **Tinned apricots** are delicious for making my Eastiest Fruity Chicken dish (see page 26). They also make a splendid base for a fruit crumble when you've run out of fresh fruit.

Required **jars** for the cupboard include a jar of runny **honey,** which keeps for a long time and is useful for making a sauce for ice-cream or for drizzling over fruit or yoghurt. I also like it in a French dressing! A jar of **green pesto** sauce. This is wonderful mixed with pasta for a quick and simple meal. It also makes a good spread on toast as a herby alternative to butter. I also like to keep in a jar of **red pesto** sauce, to make the delicious Chicken in Red Pesto Sauce, (see page 65). **Tapenade** (olive paste to you and me) makes a good spread for toast with tomatoes and cheese, or mix it with eggs to make a savoury omelette.

Dried food

Rice. If, like me, you're always running out of potatoes or you often get home to find a few mouldy offerings at the bottom of the vegetable rack, rice is a great alternative. Buy a good quality brand that won't stick and be adventurous with the type, be it basmati or wild rice. You can make things more interesting by cooking rice in stock or by adding things at the end like chopped nuts, herbs and grated carrot.

Pasta. Probably the commuting cook's best friend of all. Cook it in boiling, salted water with a spoonful of oil added so it doesn't stick together. Serve it hot with pesto sauce from a jar, or have it cold in a salad, tossed in French dressing. I like it hot, with melted butter, masses of black pepper and freshly grated Parmesan cheese.

Lentils. The orange variety is not as fashionable as the brown and green Puy type, but they cook in no time at all and are wonderful for thickening soups.

Dried milk. A godsend for busy cooks who are always running out of fresh milk. You get a nice, creamy flavour too.

Dried herbs. The freeze-dried versions aren't bad, but I fear that the cook in a hurry will have little use for dried herbs, as they generally need long, slow cooking to bring out their flavour. They're OK for an emergency, but try to buy fresh herbs or cultivate your own. Most supermarkets now stock little tubs of fresh herbs which, with care, can last quite a while and they're not that pricey.

Black peppercorns. These are a must. Never be without them or a good pepper mill. I'm also a convert to freshly ground salt. Try it on vegetables and salads and you will be too.

Garlic. Try to keep fresh garlic in, but have a jar of dried powder handy too which is a reasonable substitute when you've run out.

Stock cubes. The purists will scoff, but it's not that easy making good stock when you're a busy person. I like the vegetable cubes and find them useful for soups and sauces. Always buy a good quality brand.

Olive oil. Yes, it's expensive but it really does make a difference in cooking. I cook mostly with olive oil in these recipes and I hope you can too, but it's not the end of the world if you can't and there are some good vegetable and sunflower oils on the market. Keep your most expensive extra-virgin oils for dressings and drizzling over dishes; don't waste it by using it for frying.

YOUR FREEZER

Bread. Bread freezes well and defrosts fairly quickly, so always keep a spare loaf in the freezer. You'll need it sooner or later for pâtés, soups, salads etc.

Frozen spinach. This is one of the vegetables which really does keep well in the freezer and tastes good when thawed. Buy leaves frozen in small rounds as they're much easier to defrost than big blocks.

Frozen peas. A very useful addition which cook straight from the freezer in minutes and provide lots of fibre and vitamin C. Serve with butter and black pepper and some chopped mint. Delicious!

Frozen pastry. Ready-rolled squares of puff pastry are brilliant since there's no messing around with rolling pins and floury boards. All you have to do is to remember to take them out of the freezer in advance to defrost. Put sliced tomatoes and herbs on top, drizzle over a little olive oil and you have a wonderful light meal or starter. For a delicious pudding, top with some stewed apple and raisins.

Ice cream. Why not jazz it up with chocolate sauce or fruits?

YOUR FRIDGE

Always keep **eggs** in stock. They are invaluable for quick snacks or hearty breakfasts.

Lemons. Try to have a fresh lemon in at all times too. If you served a few too many gins and tonic, then have a bottle of **lemon juice** in stock. It's not the real thing, but it's not a bad substitute. Also handy to have in is a bottle of **lime juice**, (the real stuff, not the squash). Fresh limes are increasingly available in the big stores but are not quite as ubiquitous as the lemon.

Butter keeps for ages and is always useful as is **crème fraîche**, which keeps better than ordinary cream. **Greek**

yoghurt too will sit quite happily in the fridge for a couple of weeks and more.

Cheese. I always have a small block of fresh **Parmesan** in the fridge as it lasts for ages and is the perfect topping for a pasta. Cheese like **Cheddar** is relatively easy to get hold of, but if you're shopping at a delicatessen or big supermarket, you may like to stock up on more exotic ones like **Feta** which keeps for months in the fridge and is good for salads and Pasta Feta (see page 54); or **Halloumi** cheese, which also keeps well and is lovely fried in olive oil with a herby dressing over the top (see page 45).

If you don't have any fresh herbs in pots, try to keep a bunch of **spring onions** in your fridge. They're invaluable since you can substitute the tops for chives and the bulbs for onions.

These are some of the basics I like to have in but the list could be a lot longer depending on your culinary fancies. For example, if you cook a lot with **ginger,** you may like to keep a jar of chopped ginger in the fridge or a lump of root ginger in the freezer which will grate directly without thawing. Or if you like stir-fries, keep a bottle of **soy sauce** in the cupboard. If you're a quiche person, get some cooked, plain **pastry cases** which will sit quite happily in the cupboard until you want to fill them. If you like puddings, keep in a jar of **apple compote** and it will always come in useful.

Finally, in an ideal world, we would only ever use fresh ingredients, but, as we know, life is not always ideal. So, use fresh ingredients if possible, but don't panic if you can't.

YOUR EQUIPMENT

You might think a busy cook would need a lot of gadgets to speed up the process, but you don't need a lot of equipment. What you do have should be handy and not out of reach on a top shelf or hidden away in a cupboard, otherwise you'll never use it.

Everyone has a tale of their worst buy. Mine is an ice-cream maker which I saw in a store and had to have, otherwise my life, never mind my kitchen, would not be complete. I had, I suppose, visions of jumping off the train and throwing in some fruit and cream and producing gourmet puds. Well, I was wrong, because in the five years I had it, I never used it once. I eventually gave it to my mother and she loves it and uses it regularly. However, she is not a commuting cook.

So don't rush to buy something you probably won't use.

What you ought to have in your kitchen is the following:

A set of good **weighing scales**. Some people guess the amounts, for example, my grandma. But then after 80 years of cooking she is entitled to. You will need a **tablespoon** for measuring. The standard measure for a tablespoon is 15 ml and 3 teaspoons make a tablespoon. Always have a **measuring jug** for rice and liquids.

A decent **garlic press** is a good investment, otherwise it'll drive you mad trying to get the bits out of a not-so-good one. The press may also have an arm for taking the stones out of olives and cherries. A **cooking brush** and a really good, sharp pair of **kitchen scissors**, which are very useful for snipping chives, bacon, sun-dried tomatoes and the like. Don't skimp when you buy a **decent sharp knife** since you always get what you pay for. A **grater** for cheese and lemon rind is essential. You'll be using it in a hurry so be careful it's not one that's going to catch your fingers. **Foil** is useful for cooking and covering, as is **clingfilm.**

Other necessary luxuries include an **electric mixer.** I whipped some cream by hand the other day and I must have been mad since it took me ten minutes and left me aching! So use your electric mixer for whipping cream and eggs and keep it within reach or the sheer effort of getting it out will mean you don't.

If you're fortunate, you'll have a **food processor**. Again, keep it out on the worktop or you won't use it. I use mine for making dips, smoothing sauces, puréeing soups and for shredding large amounts of vegetables like cabbage.

A **microwave** really can be your best friend, so much so that I've given it a chapter all to itself later in the book.

If you're a forgetful cook, and you're entitled to be after a fraught journey home, a **timer** may be the answer. Get one with a clear bell or buzzer!

And one *real* help for the commuting cook is a family who will willingly and happily wash up. If that isn't the case and you can possibly afford it and have the room, get a **dishwasher**. I adore the cooking. It's the mess afterwards that I can't get to grips with.

Just a few more notes on getting ready to cook. Preparation time allows you to gather together ingredients, open tins, whip up cream, etc. Unfortunately it cannot take into account rushing to the shops to buy something you've forgotten in mid-recipe. So learn to juggle your time and above all, know your kitchen and the contents of your fridge, freezer and food cupboards.

I have given preparation times for all the recipes, but they are just a rough guide, since some cooks are faster than others and obviously, if you've just come in from work and are tired, you'll be moving more slowly. The cooking time, too, may vary very slightly since some ovens are hotter than others and some gas rings more intense.

Remember to be resourceful. If a recipe calls for butter and garlic and herbs, try to buy a tub of butter with garlic and herbs already in it. If another requires peaches and you only have nectarines, use those instead! If you need self-raising flour and you only have plain, add a teaspoon of baking powder to the plain and hope for the best. In short, cheat where you can and it will probably go unnoticed!

Finally, enjoy it! Cooking, even for the commuting cook, should be fun...

Easy, Easy, Easy...

These recipes are for when you haven't got any time at all. They are simple, quick and tasty and can be pre-pared in an instant, so there are no excuses! Preparation and cooking times range between five and fifteen minutes for all these dishes, with the exception of the Easiest Bread.

EASIEST OIL DRESSING

6 tbsp olive oil
¹/₂ level tsp French mustard
1 tbsp white wine vinegar
1 tsp runny honey
Freshly ground salt and black pepper

Put everything in a screw-top jar, put the lid on tightly and shake well until it's all mixed.

Note: if you've no honey, then add a quarter of a teaspoon of caster sugar instead. You can also vary things by adding a spoonful of chopped herbs, or a clove of crushed garlic. Or how about using a different flavoured vinegar, for example, tarragon vinegar, or changing the mustard and using a coarse grain?

EASIEST CREAMY DRESSING

4oz/115g fromage frais
6 sun-dried tomatoes in oil, drained
Freshly ground salt and black pepper

Put fromage frais and tomatoes in a food processor and whizz until smooth.

Adjust seasoning and serve with raw vegetables or a crisp lettuce heart.

Note: if you don't have a processor, use a couple of table-spoons of pesto sauce instead of the tomatoes and stir everything together by hand.

Serves 4.

EASIEST DIP

3oz/85g jar tapenade (olive paste)
1 tbsp olive oil
7oz/200g low fat cream cheese
1 tbsp lemon juice
Freshly ground salt and black pepper

With a potato masher, mash olive paste, olive oil, lemon juice and cream cheese until smooth. Adjust seasoning and eat with raw vegetables or warm pieces of pitta bread.

Serves 4.

EASIEST SUMMER SOUP

35 fl oz or 1½ pints/1 litre of chilled tomato juice
6 tbsp French dressing
1 handful chives, snipped
Freshly ground salt and black pepper

Mix the tomato juice and dressing and season with salt and pepper. Serve cold immediately, with the chives and more ground pepper sprinkled over the top, or return to the fridge until ready to garnish and serve.

Serves 4.

Note: this soup can be further enhanced by the addition of tiny cubes of cucumber or tomato ... *if* you have the time!

EASIEST WINTER SOUP

14oz/400g tinned creamed sweetcorn
5 fl oz/150ml chicken or vegetable stock
5 fl oz/150ml milk
1 handful chives and parsley, chopped
1 tbsp lemon juice
Freshly ground salt and black pepper

Put everything in a pan and bring gently to the boil, then simmer until heated through.
Serves 3-4.

EASIEST VEGETABLE STARTER

14oz/400g tinned flageolet beans, drained and rinsed
3 tbsp olive oil
1 tbsp lemon juice
1 tbsp fresh herbs, chopped — tarragon or chives are
nice, but mint gives a different and delicious flavour
1 clove garlic, crushed
Freshly ground salt and black pepper

Mix beans, oil, lemon, herbs and garlic. Do it carefully, so the beans don't all break up. Season well with salt and black pepper and serve with crusty bread.
Serves 3.

EASIEST HOT FISH STARTER

3 x 4oz/115g tinned sardines in oil
2 tbsp grainy mustard
1 lemon, quartered
Freshly ground black pepper

Heat the grill until piping hot. Drain the sardines and smear mustard over each one. Grill for three to four minutes until crispy and hot. Season with lots of black pepper and a squeeze of lemon juice.
Serves 4

EASIEST FISH PÂTÉ

4oz/115g cream cheese with chives
6oz/170g can kipper fillets in oil, drained
1 heaped tsp creamy horseradish sauce
1 tbsp lemon juice
Freshly ground salt and black pepper

Mash everything together and season well. Alternatively, put everything in the food processor and whizz for a few seconds.
Serves 3-4

EASIEST PASTA No 1

12oz/350g dried pasta
3oz/85g small jar pesto sauce
2oz/55g butter
Freshly ground salt and black pepper

Cook pasta as directed. Drain it well and put it back on a gentle heat. Add the butter and the pesto and stir everything quickly around until the butter melts and things are heated through.

Grind over lots of black pepper and serve.

Serves 4.

EASIEST PASTA No 2

Use recipe for Easiest Pasta No 1, but instead of the pesto, add a 200g carton of cream cheese with garlic and herbs. Stir it carefully into the hot, drained pasta with 2 table-spoons of milk until the cheese melts. Add lots of black pepper.

EASIEST SALAD

2 Midget Gem lettuces
2 tbsp lemon-flavoured fromage frais
2 tbsp mayonnaise
2 tbsp chives or spring onion tops, snipped
Freshly ground salt and black pepper

Remove outer leaves from lettuce and cut off woody stalks. Slice each lettuce lengthways into quarters. Take four plates and put two quarter lettuces on each plate. Sprinkle over the chives or onion tops.

Mix the fromage frais and mayonnaise and put a dollop of this dressing on the side of each plate. Grind salt and black pepper over the top and serve.

Serves 4.

Note: the beauty of this lettuce is that it generally doesn't need washing, as long as you take off the outer leaves. However, do check before you put them on the plate. If you can't get lemon-flavoured fromage frais, use the plain type and add a teaspoon of lemon juice, or try something exotic and use apricot or raspberry fromage frais instead.

EASIEST FISH DISH

4 pieces of cod, each approx 6oz/170g and 1 inch thick
2 tbsp lime juice
2 tbsp plain flour
1 clove garlic, crushed
2 tbsp olive oil
Freshly ground salt and black pepper

Mix the crushed garlic with the lime juice. Meanwhile, put the flour onto a plate and add some salt and pepper to season it. Next, dip the fish into the lime juice and then press it into the flour, so both sides gets nicely covered.

Heat the olive oil in a frying pan and fry the fish gently until it's nicely browned and starting to crisp a little. It will take three to four minutes for each side.

Add an extra squeeze of lime — and more black pepper and salt, if needed.

Serves 4.

Note: fresh dill snipped over the top of this is delicious! If you don't have lime, use lemon.

EASIEST FISH PASTA

12oz/350g dried pasta
12oz/350g jar of mussels in tomato and vegetable
    sauce, called 'mussels provençale'
Parmesan cheese, grated
Freshly ground salt and black pepper

Cook pasta according to instructions. Drain and put back on a gentle heat. Add the contents of the jar and mix carefully round until heated through.

Eat with lots of ground black pepper and the Parmesan sprinkled over the top.

Serves 4.

EASIEST VEGETARIAN DISH

12oz/350g button mushrooms
3oz/85g tub butter with garlic and herbs
1 tbsp extra fresh herbs, chopped, such as chives
2 tbsp lemon juice
Freshly ground salt and black pepper

Melt the garlic and herb butter in a wide frying pan and fry the mushrooms quickly for four to five minutes, tossing them about so they all get evenly coated.

Add the lemon juice and serve with black pepper and herbs sprinkled over the top. Eat with crusty bread.

Serves 3-4

EASIEST FRUITY CHICKEN DISH

4 chicken breasts, skinned and cut in quarters
15oz/425g tin good quality French onion soup
12 canned apricots (from a tin of fruit in juice, not
   syrup)
1oz/30g butter
Freshly ground salt and black pepper

Melt the butter in a wide saucepan, or deep frying pan, and quickly brown the chicken breast halves on both sides.

While they're browning, roughly mash the apricots with a potato masher, and mix with the onion soup and a little black pepper.

Next, pour this mixture over the chicken in the pan. Bring to the boil and cover with a lid and cook gently for 15 minutes, turning the chicken over half-way through the cooking time.

Adjust seasoning and serve.

Serves 4.

EASIEST CREAMY CHICKEN DISH

1lb/450g chicken, cut into strips
2oz/55g butter
3 tbsp dry sherry
10 fl oz/300ml double cream
1 tbsp herbs, chopped — e.g., parsley, chives, tarragon
Freshly ground salt and black pepper

Heat the butter and quickly fry the chicken strips for four minutes, tossing from side to side until they are slightly browned.

Add salt and pepper and remove from the pan to a warm dish. Pour the sherry into the pan and stir well to get all the flavours from the pan then add the cream and herbs and stir well until the mixture starts to boil. Adjust seasoning, reduce

26

the heat and put the chicken strips back in the sauce. Cook gently for two minutes and serve.

Serves 4.

EASIEST MEAT DISH

1lb/450g pork escalopes
2oz/55g butter
2 tbsp olive oil
2 tsp fresh sage leaves, chopped (or 1 tsp dried)
1 tbsp lemon juice
Freshly ground salt and black pepper

Melt butter and olive oil until sizzling and add pork and sage. Cook quickly for four minutes, turning the meat over halfway through, so it gets nicely browned on each side.

Next, add the lemon juice and salt and pepper and give it all a gentle mix round and serve.

Serves 4.

EASIEST COLD PUDDING
(TO MAKE IN ADVANCE...)

10 fl oz/300ml double cream
3 chocolate Flake bars
3 tbsp orange liqueur

Whip cream until thick but not stiff. Crumble the Flakes and add to the cream. Next, gently stir in the liqueur.

Spoon it into a glass dish or dishes. If not making in advance, leave it for ten minutes before eating.

Serves 4

Note: other spirits will do just as well here — for example, a coffee liqueur would be delicious.

EASIEST COLD PUDDING
(TO EAT AT ONCE...)

4 ripe bananas
10 fl oz/300ml creamy Greek yoghurt
1oz/30g icing sugar

Mash the bananas with a potato masher until smooth and

mix with the yoghurt. Spoon into four dishes and sieve the icing sugar evenly over the top.

Serves 4.

Note: if you have a food processor, simply whizz the fruit and yoghurt together.

EASIEST FOOD PROCESSOR PUDDING
(THANK YOU, SARAH HAMMOND!)

3 large, ripe Kiwi fruits, peeled
1oz/30g caster sugar
10 fl oz/300ml double cream, whipped
A few drops vanilla essence

Blend the Kiwi fruits and sugar in the food processor until smooth. Mix with cream and vanilla essence and serve.

Serves 4.

EASIEST HOT ALCOHOLIC PUDDING

1lb/450g ripe, juicy plums, stoned and halved
3oz/85g butter
3 tbsp Amaretto liqueur

Melt the butter in a wide frying pan and fry the plums gently on both sides for two minutes. Next add liqueur and mix gently around. Serve with the buttery juices poured over.

Serves 4.

EASIEST HOT NON-ALCOHOLIC PUDDING

4 x 5 inch/12.5cm ready-rolled sheets of puff pastry
1lb/450g jar Bonne Maman caramelised apple compote
3oz/85g raisins

Preheat the oven to gas mark 7/220C/425F. Put a greased baking tray in to heat through. Divide the apple compote between the pastry sheets, leaving a half-inch gap around the edge. Next, sprinkle raisins over the top.

Place the pastry sheets carefully on the hot tray, using a fish slice to lift them. Bake for 12-15 minutes and serve with custard or cream.

Serves 4.

Note: I've chosen Bonne Maman because it's so delicious — but you can use other makes of cooked apple, or even, Heaven forbid, make your own!

EASIEST HOT SWEET SAUCE
(FOR ICE-CREAM, ETC ...)

14oz/400g canned black cherries in syrup
3 tbsp Kirsch

Gently heat the liqeur, fruit (and the syrup they come in) in a pan and serve.
Serves 4

EASIEST COLD SWEET SAUCE

6 very ripe Kiwi fruits, peeled
3oz/85g caster sugar

Put the Kiwi fruits and the sugar in the food processor and whizz until smooth. This sauce will sit quite happily in the fridge until needed.
Serves 4.
Note: if you don't have a processor, purée the Kiwi fruits by pushing them through a sieve with a wooden spoon and mix in the sugar by hand.

EASIEST BREAD

Yes, believe it or not, there is an easy-to-make bread. My mother, who has made bread all her life, says this is definitely one requring minimum effort! Although it takes a while to cook, it needs no proving or kneading. In fact, the only difficult bit might be finding all the right ingredients!

This bread is famous in London's Primrose Hill and is the recipe of Clare Latimer. I found it in the London *Evening Standard* newspaper, which of course, is known by commuters throughout the South-east. I do hope that they, or she, won't mind me giving it to you.

6oz/170g wholemeal flour
2oz/55g white flour
2oz/55g pinhead oatmeal

2oz/55g wheatgerm
2oz/55g bran
2oz/55g pecan nuts, chopped
1 tsp bicarbonate of soda
$\frac{1}{2}$ tsp salt
1 tsp sugar
1 egg
10 fl oz/300ml skimmed milk
A little butter for greasing

Preheat the oven to gas mark 5/190C/375F. Grease a 2 pint/40 fl oz/1.1l loaf tin.

Mix all the dry ingredients in a large bowl. Next add the milk and the egg and stir around until everything is well-mixed.

Bake in the oven for 45-60 minutes. It's ready when a sharp knife or skewer inserted through the middle comes out clean.

Note: You can use walnuts instead of pecans. This also freezes extremely well and must be one of the healthiest breads around — just think of all that fibre!

Journey's Start...

...JULY 1992 — FOURTEEN WOMEN COMMUTERS ARE TO GET COMPENSATION AFTER BEING LOCKED IN AN EMPTY TRAIN AND PUT INTO THE SIDINGS FOR SEVERAL HOURS.

Yes, even a commuting cook sometimes needs a starter — and really, in these days of ready-mixed salad leaves and pre-washed vegetables, it's not that difficult. You may need to do a bit of chopping and stirring, but as Nigel Slater asks in his wonderful book, *Real Fast Food*: 'Can anyone really be too busy to slice a courgette?'

Essentials to have when you do make the effort are a bottle of quality olive oil and some fresh lemons, because these two on their own can make a wonderfully simple dressing for salads and vegetable starters. Drizzle over a bit of oil, squeeze on a little lemon juice and top with lots of freshly ground salt and black pepper and you're ready to eat.

Having said that, a basic **French dressing** is terribly easy to make. Just pop three parts of olive oil, one part of white wine vinegar, one teaspoon of coarse-grain French mustard and a sprinkle of dried basil into a jar, put the lid on, give it all a good shake and it will keep for a week or more in the fridge. Always keep a jar of dressing handy, but if you really can't be bothered to make your own, do buy a good quality make, and then let me know what it's called!

Also very useful to have in the fridge is a small jar of **mayonnaise** because it keeps for a long time and is useful for salads and dips. I have, occasionally, been known to make my own mayonnaise, but it's a bit fiddly to do and really, whilst there are so much good quality products around, why bother?

So, once you've got your dressing, all you need are some **fresh fruit and vegetables** to make a wonderfully simple start to your meal.

For instance: slice some **tomatoes** and arrange them on a large plate; spoon over a little olive oil and add a squeeze

31

of lemon; snip some chives over the top and grind on black pepper. Eat with a chunk of crusty bread.

Top and tail **green beans** and cook for a couple of minutes in boiling, salted water. If they've seen fresher days, pop in a vegetable stock cube to give them a little more flavour. Serve drained and warm, with a well-flavoured French dressing and freshly milled salt and pepper. Snip any herbs you have — e.g., parsley or chervil, over the top.

Or what about a **cauliflower**? One of the meals I especially remember was just that and nothing else. It was 15 years ago in a garden in the south of France and I can taste it still: a freshly picked cauliflower, cooked but still firm and divided into florets. It was served slightly warm with a dressing of olive oil, garlic and lemon and it was magnificent!

Bags of **pre-washed mixed salad leaves** which can be bought ready for use are a godsend for the commuting cook. Simply turn them out into a bowl and serve with a dressing, or sprinkled with a handful of pinenuts or some croutons, a few slices of apple or avocado or some sliced mushrooms. I like to serve dressed salad leaves with slivers of Parmesan cheese and a few nuts. There are very few rules about salads, but freshness is definitely one of them.

Mushrooms make wonderfully quick starters. Buy tiny button ones and fry them quickly for a couple of minutes in garlic butter. Buy the garlic butter ready-made and save yourself a job! Alternatively, slice mushrooms thinly and mix with washed, young spinach leaves torn into pieces. Toss it all in a well-flavoured lemon and olive oil dressing, add lots of freshly ground black pepper and sprinkle with chopped chives or parsley. Or buy some big field mushrooms and brush them with olive oil. Squeeze over some fresh garlic and grill for a few minutes.

Thinly slice a couple of **courgettes** and mix with diced **Edam** or **Mozzarella** cheese. Add a handful of olives and a couple of spoons of French dressing and top with chopped herbs and freshly ground pepper.

Or another favourite — the good old **avocado.** Soft and buttery, serve it on its own, with just a squeeze of lemon juice and a turn of black pepper. If you've a little more time, peel and slice it, then serve on a plate with sliced tomatoes. Alternate the slices, so that it looks pretty and spoon some French dressing over the top. Finish with a sprinkling of fresh basil leaves, or — and this is one of my all-time favourites — overlapping slices of avocado, tomato *and* Mozzarella, all dressed and ready to go.

Avocados are so versatile. They can be mashed and

mixed with lemon juice and Tabasco to make a tasty dip. They can be wrapped, perhaps in slices of smoked salmon or ultra-thin parma ham. They can also be filled with all sorts of goodies; an egg perhaps, hard-boiled and chopped and mixed with a couple of tablespoons of good quality mayonnaise; a spoonful of **hummous** or a handful of juicy **prawns.**

Something else just waiting to be dressed and filled is a **melon.** Buy a small, sweet one, halve it and scoop out the seeds and fill with a couple of spoonfuls of French dressing. For something more exotic, serve it filled with fresh **raspberries** or tiny cubes of Edam cheese and seedless **grapes.** Or make a filling of crumbled **Stilton** and chopped, **smoked ham.** Mix it with French dressing on workdays, and at the weekend go mad with a spoonful of port.

A sweet **pear** can be halved, peeled, cored and topped with a slice of **Dolcelatte** or **goat's cheese.** Pop it under a hot grill for a few seconds until the cheese starts to bubble and brown and you have a deliciously simple starter. Serve it on lettuce leaves which have been tossed in a walnut oil and lemon dressing and scatter some chopped walnuts over the top and you've a light main meal.

Tinned beans make great starters. Rinse and drain a can of flageolots and mix them with 2 tbsp of lemon juice and 4 tbsp olive oil. Add a crushed garlic clove and some seasoning and serve on a crisp Webb's lettuce leaf.

Mix a tin of pinto beans with some thinly sliced mushrooms and a couple of chopped spring onions. Stir in a half-yoghurt, half-mayonnaise dressing and serve with lots of black pepper. Or simply purée the beans in the processor and mix with garlic, lemon juice and seasoning to produce a delicious dip for pitta bread or sliced raw vegetables.

Use **tinned fish,** for example, **tuna** or **salmon,** to make quick pâtés. Simply drain the can and mash with a carton of cream cheese, or alternatively, pop the whole lot in the processor and whizz for a few seconds. Add salt and pepper and serve with small gherkins and hot, buttered toast. The calorie conscious may like to use fromage frais instead of cream cheese.

Tuna mixed with drained, tinned beans and a French dressing is delicious. Add any chopped herbs you've got. If you've more time, add pieces of lettuce, and some chopped tomatoes, onion and boiled egg and you've got a form of **salade Niçoise.** Use olives and chopped parsley for real effect.

Sardines, packed in oil, are a wonderful standby. Drain and mash with cream cheese, add lemon juice and seasoning to make a sardine pâté. Or simply drain and dry them and pop onto an oiled baking tray. Smear French or wholegrain mustard over the tops and cook for a couple of minutes under a hot grill. Serve with a squeeze of lemon and imagine you're by the sea...

Another useful fish, not tinned but with a reasonably long shelf life is **smoked mackerel**. Keep it in the fridge and you'll find that, either plain or peppered, it makes a delicious and most acceptable starter. Serve it cold, but not freezing, with wedges of lemon. Or heat it gently under the grill for a couple of minutes and serve on buttered toast.

And finally, there is that wonderful starter standby —the **egg**! Serve it baked — just break an egg into a buttered ramekin dish and season with salt and pepper, add a spoonful of single cream and cook in a moderate oven (gas mark 5 190C/375F) for ten minutes or so.

Or for a more exotic and expensive start to the meal, serve them scrambled with strips of Scotch smoked salmon.

But for the simplest egg starter of them all — remember the days when everybody made egg mayonnaise? Bring them back! Just boil the eggs, one per person, cool, shell and halve them and place them on a bed of lettuce. Cover with a couple of spoons of good quality mayonnaise and snip a few chives over the top and I can guarantee that if you've got folk round to supper, someone will say — 'Egg mayonnaise! I haven't had that for years!'

COLD STARTERS

TWO-PEAR PLATE

Preparation time: 10 minutes
Cooking time: none

2 ripe avocado pears, peeled, halved and stoned and cut lengthways into quarter-inch slices.
2 ripe sweet pears, peeled, cored and halved and cut lengthways into quarter-inch slices.
4 tbsp French dressing
Freshly ground black pepper

Try to get both avocado and sweet pears the same size.
Using half an avocado pear and half a sweet pear for each plate, arrange alternative slices of sweet and avocado pear in

a fan-shape on four plates,

Drizzle some French dressing over the finished dish and grind on some black pepper.

Serves 4.

Note: this is equally good made with melon instead of sweet pear. If you are really rushing, don't bother about cutting the fruit. Simply arrange both halves of pear boldly next to each other and look confident as you serve!

IN A HURRY HUMMOUS

Preparation time: 10 minutes
Cooking time: none, but a food processor is needed.

This can be made the night before and kept, covered, in the fridge.

14oz/400g canned chick peas, rinsed and drained
1 tbsp lemon juice
2 cloves garlic, peeled
3 tbsp sesame oil
2 tbsp olive oil
Freshly ground salt and black pepper

Put the chick peas into a food processor with the lemon juice and garlic. Whizz the whole lot for 30 seconds or so, and when it's all smooth, slowly trickle both the oils through the funnel, still whizzing as you do so.

Add seasoning to taste and serve with hot toast and butter or warm pitta bread.

Serves 4.

Note: the lemon in this is a personal thing. You may like to add a little more, but taste it first.

CORIANDER BEAN MIX

14oz/400g canned white haricot beans, drained and rinsed
7oz/200g tinned tuna in oil, drained and flaked
3 spring onions
1 tbsp fresh coriander, chopped
4 tbsp French dressing
Freshly ground salt and black pepper

Put the beans, tuna and coriander into a bowl and mix gently around.

With a pair of scissors, snip the green tops of the spring onions into the salad. Quarter the onion bulbs and add these too to the bowl. Add the dressing and mix everything around gently. Season and serve.

Serves 4.

Note: this is nice served on a crisp lettuce leaf. If you can't get fresh coriander, use chives or parsley instead.

GREEK LEEK STARTER

Preparation time: 10-15 minutes
Cooking time: 15 minutes

The leeks can be cooked in advance and kept covered and cool. Assemble with the mushrooms and cheese when ready to eat.

4 firm leeks, washed, approximately 1 inch/2.5cm in diameter and 6 inches/15cm long
4 large field mushrooms
2 tbsp olive oil
7oz/200g Feta cheese cubes from a jar of Patros Feta in oil.
Dressing, made with 4 tbsp oil from the cheese jar and 1 tbsp lemon juice
Freshly ground salt and black pepper

Cook the leeks in boiling, well-salted water for five to seven minutes or until tender. Meanwhile fry the mushrooms in the olive oil for a couple of minutes on each side. You want both vegetables to be cooked, but not soggy.

When the leeks are tender, drain them on a clean tea towel and leave them to cool. Allow the mushrooms to cool too. When ready to eat, put out four plates. Cut each leek in half, lengthways, and arrange two leek halves and one whole mushroom on each plate.

Pile the cubes of drained Feta cheese over the vegetables. Spoon over the oil and lemon dressing and season to taste.

Serves 4.

Note: if you can't find Patros Feta in oil, cube a chunk of ordinary Feta cheese and make the dressing using olive oil and lemon juice.

SMOKED MACKEREL MOUSSE

Preparation time: 5-10 minutes
Cooking time: none, but you need a food processor.

This is good made the night before and kept, covered, in the fridge.

10oz/285g boneless smoked mackerel, skinned
7oz/200g cream cheese
2 tbsp natural yoghurt or cream
1 tbsp creamed horseradish
Juice of ½ lemon
Freshly ground salt and black pepper

Put everything in the processor and whizz until smooth. If time permits, chill for half an hour. If not, eat straight away with buttered toast.
Serves 4-6.

STILTON PÂTÉ

Preparation time: 10 minutes, less with a food processor
Cooking time: none

Again, good made the night before and kept, covered, in the fridge

6oz/170g Stilton cheese
7oz/200g tub cream cheese
2oz/55g softened butter
1 eggcupful of port
2oz/55g walnuts, chopped roughly
Freshly ground black pepper

Put everything apart from the walnuts into the processor and whizz for 30 seconds or so, or until smooth. Mix in the nuts by hand. Adjust seasoning and eat with raw vegetables or oatcakes.
Serves 4-6
Note: if you haven't got a processor, mix everything together with a potato masher, again adding the nuts separately at the end.

TWO-FISH PÂTÉ

Preparation time: 10 minutes, less with a food processor
Cooking time: none

This is good made the night before and kept, covered, in the fridge.

7oz/200g tinned tuna in oil, drained
5oz/150g medium-fat cream cheese
1 tbsp lemon juice
2 tsp anchovy essence
2 tbsp gherkins, chopped
Freshly ground salt and black pepper

If doing it by hand, mash the fish well with a fork. Next mix in the lemon juice, the essence, the cream cheese and the gherkins. Add salt and pepper to taste.

Alternatively pop everything, except the gherkins, into a food processor and whizz until smooth. Mix in the gherkins by hand at the end.

Serves 4.

LAURA'S SPINACH PÂTÉ

Preparation time: 15 minutes — you need a food processor
Cooking time: 5 minutes

Again, good made the night before and kept, covered, in the fridge.

8oz/225g cold cooked spinach
1 small onion, grated
1 tin anchovies, drained
2 eggs, hard-boiled (see page 115)
4oz/115g butter, melted
1 tbsp lemon juice
Freshly ground salt and black pepper

Put the eggs on to boil for 8-10 minutes since you want them hard-boiled. Meanwhile, melt the butter, add the onion and cook that gently for two to three minutes, or until soft.

Next, shell the eggs and place in a food processor with the spinach, onion and butter, anchovies and lemon juice. Blend until everything is smooth. Adjust seasoning. If you

have time, chill for a while. If not, eat at once with toast.
Serves 4-6.
Note: I often use a bag of frozen spinach for this recipe, but do allow it to defrost properly before you mix it with the melted butter or you'll have a disaster!

RIGHT LEAF SALAD

You know how the trains sometimes can't run because of leaves on the line? No problem with these little beauties ...

Preparation time: 10 minutes
Cooking time: none

8oz/225g bag mixed lettuce leaves
8 rashers streaky bacon, snipped into quarter-inch
  pieces
1 tbsp olive oil
4oz/115g mushrooms, wiped and thinly sliced
3 tbsp French dressing
Freshly ground salt and black pepper

Divide the leaves onto four plates.
Heat the olive oil and fry the bacon quickly for two to three minutes or until it's starting to crisp slightly.
Next add the mushrooms and cook quickly for a further minute.
Divide the mushrooms and bacon between the salads.
Spoon over the dressing. Season to taste and serve *at once* or it will go soggy.
Note: You can add croutons to this dish or bits of chopped avocado, or a few pinenuts. You may also like to save time by buying ready-chopped bacon bits. If you do snip your own, use a pair of scissors to do it — it's much quicker.

TOMATO, OLIVE AND COURGETTE SALAD

Preparation time: 10-15 minutes
Cooking time: none

2 medium-sized courgettes, trimmed and thinly sliced
4 medium tomatoes, sliced
16 olives, black or green, pitted and left whole
2 tbsp fresh herbs, chopped, such as parsley, chives

4 tbsp olive oil
2 tsp lemon juice
1 tbsp pesto sauce
Freshly ground salt and black pepper

First of all, make the dressing. Put the olive oil, lemon juice, pesto sauce and salt into a jar. Put the lid on and shake it well. Taste and season with salt and pepper. Arrange the courgettes and the tomatoes on a plate. Sprinkle over the herbs and scatter on the olives. Drizzle over the dressing and grind on more black pepper.
Serves 4.

AVOCADO DIP

Preparation time: 10 minutes
Cooking time: none

2 ripe avocados, halved and stoned
2 tbsp lemon juice
1 tbsp olive oil
1 small bunch of chives, finely snipped
1 tsp Worcester sauce
Freshly ground salt and black pepper

Spoon out the flesh from the avocado and mash it with a potato masher until smooth. Next, carefully mix in all the other ingredients and serve with raw vegetables or fingers of toast.
Serves 4.

COLD CUCUMBER SOUP

Preparation time: 5-10 minutes, with a food processor
Cooking time: none

Can be made in advance and kept, covered, in the fridge.

1 large cucumber, peeled and deseeded
5 fl oz/150 ml single cream
8oz/225g creamy plain yoghurt
1 heaped tbsp mint, chopped
2 tsp lemon juice
A few tbsp milk, to thin the soup
Freshly ground salt and black pepper

Put the cucumber in a food processor with all the other ingredients and whizz for 30 seconds or so. If it seems too thick, add a little bit of milk. Adjust seasoning and serve cold, with a couple of whole mint leaves on the top for decoration. For an extra-special exotic alternative add thinly sliced strawberries, cut from top to bottom to produce heart shapes and place on top with the mint leaves.

Serves 4.

HOT STARTERS

It's on a cold, wet winter's night that something warming really does become the commuter's friend. After huddling on that windy platform waiting for the 18.20 p.m. train, or battling your way out of the city in near-stationary traffic, a steaming bowl of soup can be a little piece of paradise...

I reckon I can make a pan of delicious soup in half an hour, which may seem like a long time to the time-pressed cook, but just imagine: you arrive home, you get it on the go, you have a shower, get changed and by the time you're sorted out, your soup's just about ready. Alternatively, make it the night before and leave it in the fridge until you need it. Most soups taste better the day after, anyway.

LENTIL AND LEMON SOUP

Preparation time: 5-10 minutes
Cooking time: 25 minutes

2¹/₂ pints/1.5 litres homemade vegetable or chicken stock, or ...
2¹/₂ pints/1.5 litres water and 2 stock cubes; chicken or vegetable
6 heaped tbsp red lentils (these don't need soaking ...)
1 medium onion, chopped finely
1¹/₂ tbsp lemon juice
Small handful chopped parsley or chives
Freshly ground salt and black pepper

First of all, you need to boil your stock. If you're using water, boil it in the kettle for extra speed and transfer it to the saucepan. Once the water is boiling, that's the time to add the stock cubes.

Now tip in the lentils and the onion and simmer for 20-25 minutes. If it becomes too thick add a little more water.

Adjust the seasoning, add lemon juice and finish with the herbs and ground black pepper on the top.

Serves 4.

Note: this is a low-fat soup with lots of fibre! And it can be made a couple of days in advance as it really does improve with age. Commuting cooks with slightly more time could add a grated carrot along with the onions and lentil.

CAULIFLOWER AND THYME SOUP

Preparation time: 10 minutes, with a food processor
Cooking time: 20 minutes

Part of this can be made in advance and kept, covered, in the fridge until ready to complete the recipe.

1 medium cauliflower, the florets only
1 onion, peeled and quartered
2oz/55g butter
1½ pints/900ml well-flavoured vegetable stock (if using stock cubes, use 2)
5floz/150ml pot single cream
1 tbsp fresh thyme leaves or 1 tsp dried
2oz/55g Gruyère cheese
Freshly ground salt and black pepper

Chop the onion in the food processor.

Next add the cauliflower florets and whizz until you have cauliflower crumbs. Melt the butter and stir the cauliflower and onion crumbs quickly around until all the butter is soaked up.

Now add the stock and the thyme and bring everything to the boil. Allow to simmer for 15 minutes. If making this in advance, stop here, allow to cool, and leave, covered, in the fridge.

When you are ready to eat, reheat, add the cream and the cheese and stir around until the cheese melts.

Adjust seasoning and serve.

Serves 4.

Note: this is a meal in itself. Eat with chunks of fresh bread. This recipe works well with broccoli florets instead of cauliflower, but you will only need to cook it for 10 minutes instead of 15. For a quick Carrot and Coriander soup, use 1lb/0.5kg of carrots instead of cauliflower. Peel, top and tail the carrots and shred them in the processor. Follow the recipe above but instead of thyme leaves, use coriander. Commuting cooks can always buy their carrots in a bag, ready-shredded.

MINTY TOMATO SOUP

Preparation time: 10 minutes
Cooking time: 15 minutes

2 x 14oz/400g canned chopped tomatoes
1 medium onion, grated
2oz/55g butter
1 pt/575 ml well-flavoured vegetable stock (if using cubes, use 2)
2 tbsp mint leaves, chopped
4 tbsp creamy natural yoghurt
Freshly ground salt and black pepper

Melt the butter in a pan and add the onion. Cook gently for two minutes, stirring around so it doesn't burn.

Next add the tomatoes and the stock, bring everything to the boil and simmer for ten minutes. When it's almost ready, stir in the mint.

If you have time, purée the soup. If not, eat it chunky and simply adjust the seasoning and serve with a spoonful of yoghurt swirled over the top of each serving.

Serves 4.

Note: for Basil Tomato Soup, add a handful of chopped basil. For Herby Tomato Soup, use tinned, chopped tomatoes with herbs.

HERBED PEA SOUP

Preparation time: 5-10 minutes
Cooking time: 10 minutes

8oz/225g packet frozen peas
4oz/115g cream cheese and chives
1/2 pint/300ml milk
1/2 pint/300ml vegetable stock

Put the frozen peas in the stock. Bring to the boil and cook gently for five minutes. Allow to cool slightly and put into a food processor with the cream cheese. Whizz until smooth and return to pan.

Add milk until you have a soup consistency. You may not need all the milk. Adjust seasoning and serve with chopped herbs sprinkled over the top.

Serves 4.

CHEESE CHIVE SOUP

Preparation time: 10 minutes
Cooking time: 10 minutes

2oz/55g butter
2oz/55g flour
1/2 pint/300 fl oz vegetable stock
1/2 pint/300 fl oz milk
6oz/170g Cheddar cheese, grated
1 tbsp chives, snipped
Freshly ground salt and black pepper

Melt the butter in a saucepan. Add the flour and stir around until all the lumps are out. Cook for a couple of minutes.

Next, take the pan off the heat and add the stock and milk. Mix well until it's all smooth and put back on the heat. Bring to the boil, stirring all the time, until it thickens. Cook for two minutes.

Add the grated cheese and chives and cook for another minute.

Adjust seasoning and serve with crusty bread.

Serves 4.

Note: Add a grated carrot along with the cheese and chives, if you prefer.

CREAMY GARLIC MUSHROOMS

Preparation time: 5-10 minutes
Cooking time: 7 minutes

**12oz/350g small button mushrooms, wiped but left
  whole**
2oz/55g butter with garlic and herbs
7 fl oz/200ml crème fraîche
Extra 1 tbsp parsley or chives, chopped
Freshly ground salt and black pepper

Melt the butter in a saucepan and add the mushrooms and cook for four minutes over a gentle heat, stirring round so they don't burn.

Stir in the crème fraîche and the chopped herbs and season to taste. Simmer gently for a couple more minutes. Divide between four dishes and grind black pepper over the top. Eat with crusty bread.

Serves 4.

FRIED HALLOUMI CHEESE

Preparation time: 10 minutes
Cooking time: 2-3 minutes, depending on how many slices you can get in your pan at one time.

1 Halloumi cheese, approx 10oz/300g, cut into 8 slices
2 tbsp plain flour, seasoned with freshly ground salt
   and black pepper
4 tbsp olive oil
2 tbsp lemon or lime juice
1 tbsp coarse grain mustard
1 tbsp capers, drained and rinsed
1 clove garlic, crushed
2 tbsp herbs, chopped, coriander is nicest, parsley will
   do
Freshly ground salt and black pepper

First make a dressing of the lemon juice, mustard, half the olive oil, capers, garlic and salt and pepper. Next, coat each piece of cheese in the seasoned flour. Heat the remaining olive oil in a large frying pan and fry the cheese slices quickly on both sides until they're lightly browned and starting to soften.

Divide the cheeses between four plates and spoon over the dressing. Sprinkle the herbs on top and grind on sea salt and black pepper.

Serves 4.

Note: this is from a Delia Smith recipe and is delicious and foolproof, as all her recipes are! It's a particularly good one for the commuting cook because Halloumi cheese keeps quite happily in the fridge for several months. If you are very hungry, use two Halloumi cheeses and make more dressing to match.

CREAMY CHEESE EGGS

Preparation time: 15 minutes
Cooking time: 12 minutes

4oz/115g cheese, grated — Gruyère is best, Cheddar is fine
4 tbsp double cream
4 eggs
½ oz/15g butter
1 tbsp chives, snipped
Freshly ground black pepper

Preheat oven to gas mark 4/180C/350F and put the kettle on to boil.

Butter four ramekin dishes and take half of the cheese and divide it evenly between the dishes. Top this with half of the chives.

Next, break an egg into each dish, on top of the cheese and season with salt and pepper.

Spoon one tablespoon of cream on top of each egg, followed by the rest of the cheese, the remaining chives and some black pepper.

Pop the dishes in a cake tin and pour boiling water into the tin, until it comes up to the halfway mark on the ramekins. Cook in the oven for 12 minutes, or until the eggs are set.

Serves 4.

SPICY PRAWNS

Preparation time: 10 minutes
Cooking time: 8-10 minutes

8oz/225g packet cooked frozen prawns
7oz/200g canned chopped tomatoes with herbs
1 medium onion, grated
1 clove garlic, crushed
1 tbsp olive oil
2 tbsp fresh coriander, snipped
1 heaped tsp fresh ginger, grated
A squeeze of lemon juice
Freshly ground salt and black pepper

Take the prawns out of the freezer before you leave in the morning. Put them in a bowl with a squeeze of lemon juice and a sprinkling of salt, and leave them, covered, to defrost in the fridge.

When you come in at night, grate the onion and fry it in the oil for two to three minutes, or until it's soft. Next, mix in the tomatoes, garlic, coriander and ginger and a little salt and black pepper.

Finally, drain the prawns and add these, stirring them gently around for a couple of minutes or until they're warmed through.

Adjust seasoning, add a squeeze of lemon juice and serve with crusty bread.

Serves 4.

Note: I try to keep a small jar of ready-chopped, shop-bought ginger in the fridge, because it really saves time when you're rushed. It's quite concentrated though, so go easy on the amount!

POTTED HADDOCK

Preparation time: 5 minutes
Cooking time: 15-20 minutes

10oz/300g smoked haddock, flaked
7fl oz/200ml carton crème fraîche
1oz/30g butter
1 tbsp herbs, chopped such as chives, parsley
Freshly ground black pepper

Preheat oven to gas mark 6/400F/200C. Using half the butter, grease four ramekin dishes. Divide the flaked fish between the dishes. Mix the crème fraîche with the herbs, salt and black pepper and pour this over the top of the fish, dividing it between the dishes.

Top with the remaining butter — a little bit on each one. Cook for 15-20 minutes in the oven until brown and bubbling on top.

Serves 4.

Note: this is a lovely dish, but do be careful when adding salt because some smoked fish, such as bright yellow smoked haddock, can be very salty to start with. This dish can be varied by adding a teaspoon of French mustard to the crème fraîche.

HERB AND NUT MUSHROOMS

Preparation time: 5-10 minutes
Cooking time: 15 minutes

8 large field mushrooms, stalks removed and wiped
1 x 3oz/85g packet garlic and herb butter
2oz/55g Parmesan cheese, grated
2oz/55g pine nuts
1 tbsp parsley or chives, chopped
Freshly ground salt and black pepper

Preheat oven to gas mark 6/200F/400C. Place mushrooms side by side on a buttered ovenproof dish. Divide butter into eight portions and put a piece on each mushroom. Divide the cheese equally over the top and sprinkle on the nuts, herbs and some salt and black pepper.

Cook for 15 minutes and serve.

Serves 4.

Note: these are also delicious cold, especially for a summer lunch, and can be made a few hours in advance and kept covered and cool.

On the Way...

...JAPANESE POLICIES TO MINIMISE THE SOCIAL EFFECTS OF
COMMUTING BY CAR: THESE INCLUDE TRAFFIC AND PARKING
RESTRICTIONS IN CITIES, EMPLOYEE PARKING POLICIES
DESIGNED TO CURB COMMUTING IN PRIVATE CARS, REGULAR
VEHICLE INSPECTION AND DIFFICULT AND EXPENSIVE DRIVER-
LICENSING REQUIREMENTS. THE CUMULATIVE EFFECT OF THESE
POLICIES HAS BEEN TO DISCOURAGE CAR USE.

Government transport review from the 1980s.

Now we're up and running and on to the main course. My own personal favourite is **pasta.** What, I wonder, did the British commuter do before the Italians brought it over? Dried pasta is fine and there are so many different shapes and sizes to choose from, but I've learnt over the years that it's worth choosing a good quality product since you want something which isn't going to go mushy on you. I know that folk rave about fresh pasta, and one advantage is that it does cook that much faster than dried. But I like the dried type because it keeps for ages and doesn't cost a fortune.

Bear in mind that there are also 'quick-cook' pastas on the market which can be ready in just three minutes. And when you do cook it, how simple it is! Things can be hurried up by boiling the water in a kettle first and transferring it to the pan. Get the water to a rolling boil, then add some salt — I reckon on a teaspoon of salt to six pints of water — and a teaspoon of olive or vegetable oil to stop the pasta sticking together. Then pop in the pasta, stir it all around and cook for about eight minutes or however long it suggests on the packet. Towards the end of the cooking time, check to see how it's going. You want your pasta cooked but still with a bit of bite to it. It is always worth referring to the pasta manufacturer's cooking directions on the packet to avoid mishaps.

While it cooks, you can make your sauce. For the simplest

meal, drain some cooked pasta shells and melt in a couple of ounces of butter with garlic. Sprinkle over some freshly grated Parmesan cheese and some freshly ground black pepper and salt.

For another quick dish, mix four to five tablespoons of red pepper sauce (available in delis) into cooked penne. Add chopped olives and eat with masses of freshly ground black pepper.

A garlic and herb soft cheese melted into hot pasta makes an ultra-quick sauce, but for something quite rich and special, stir a teaspoon of brandy and a tablespoon of chopped herbs into a small pot of double cream. Add some ground black pepper and you've a delicious creamy sauce for tortellini or some other filled pasta shapes.

Where pasta is concerned, be inventive with your jars! Buy artichokes in oil and mix with some coloured pasta and salt and pepper. Use different flavoured oils — for example, toss cooked pasta in walnut oil and serve with chopped walnut pieces.

A quick word on Parmesan cheese. You can use the dried, ready-grated variety, but once you've tried it fresh, you won't want to go back to anything else. It is quite expensive, but a little goes a long way and a small block, well-wrapped up, will keep quite happily in the top of the fridge for several weeks.

On to other speedy main courses: well, **fish** can be quickly cooked, although I do appreciate that fresh fish is not always easily obtained. Frozen fish is a great help to the busy cook, but you may find it needs a sauce of some kind to liven up the flavour a little.

One of my old standbys is to add a tablespoon of drained, rinsed capers and some freshly ground black pepper to a couple of ounces of melted butter. Pour it over poached fish and it's delicious. Another favourite is smoked haddock with poached egg. Take the haddock out of the freezer in the morning and leave it in the fridge to defrost during the day. Then, at night, simply poach it gently in a little milk with a bay leaf and some freshly ground black pepper. Whilst it's cooking, heat up some water and poach an egg. Serve the fish topped with the egg, with a tablespoon of melted butter spooned over and some more freshly ground black pepper to finish.

Poultry, for example, chicken and turkey, can be quick and easy to prepare. Thinly sliced, both cook within minutes. Don't forget that chicken breasts can be cut into strips and cooked in sesame oil, soy sauce and beansprouts for a tasty stir-fry.

Thin slices of **pork** can be a help to the commuting cook. Fry them gently in butter and olive oil and serve well-seasoned with chopped herbs and freshly ground black pepper. If you're feeling a little more adventurous, add a heaped teaspoon of grain mustard and a couple of tablespoons of fromage frais for a spicy, creamy sauce.

Liver cooks easily and quickly — especially if you like it the French way — pink inside. We're a little squeamish in our house and tend to like ours cooked a bit more, but that only means an extra couple of minutes or so in the pan. Fry thin slices of lamb's liver in garlic butter and a handful of chopped fresh sage leaves. It will only take a few minutes. Chicken livers are also delicious served this way and those wishing to put on weight can add a small pot of double cream to the pan!

A **steak** can cook in a matter of minutes, particularly if you like it rare. Brush the meat with oil and season it well with freshly ground black pepper, then either grill or fry it in a pan. Add salt when it's cooked and make it extra special with a squeeze of lemon juice over the top.

For the non-meat eaters — and I must admit, there are times when I head that way myself — how about a delicious **vegetable nut stir-fry**? To save time, buy the vegetables ready-chopped and mix with bean sprouts and grated ginger. Heat up a tablespoon of sesame oil and fry quickly, adding a handful of roasted cashew nuts at the end.

Rice can cook within a quarter of an hour and you can add all sorts of nice things to jazz it up, such as sliced mushrooms, a grated onion, a handful of chopped herbs, a grated carrot or some frozen peas. For a simple, basic risotto, cook the rice in vegetable stock and add some, or all, of the above. For an Italian slant, mix in a couple of spoons of pesto sauce to the cooking water.

And finally, we've talked about pasta, but **dried noodles** are also useful to have in the store-cupboard, since they cook in minutes and can be served tossed in melted butter, or olive oil, with pinenuts, capers and herbs, seasoned with sea salt and freshly ground black pepper.

Enough chat, let's get on the way ...

TOMATO AND OLIVE PASTA

Preparation time: 10 minutes
Cooking time: 10-15 minutes

12oz/350g dried pasta
1 small jar, 3¹/₂oz/100g tapenade (olive paste)
10oz/285g tomatoes, diced
6 sun-dried tomatoes, snipped into small pieces, plus 1
tbsp oil from the jar.
1 tbsp olive oil
2 tbsp fresh basil, chopped
Fresh Parmesan, grated
Freshly ground salt and black pepper

Cook pasta as directed. Drain well and mix with the tapenade, tomatoes, sun-dried tomatoes,and the oil from the jar, olive oil and basil.

Put back on the heat to warm through for a minute.

Add plenty of black pepper and serve with Parmesan sprinkled over the top.

Serves 4.

PASTA PESTO BACON

Preparation time: 10 minutes:
Cooking time: 10-15 minutes

12oz/350g dried pasta
2 tbsp olive oil
2 cloves garlic, crushed
8oz/225g bacon, diced
7 fl oz/200 ml fromage frais
1 small jar, 3¹/₂oz/100g pesto sauce
Freshly ground salt and black pepper

Cook pasta as directed. Meanwhile, heat the oil in a frying pan and add the diced bacon and garlic and cook for five minutes, stirring around to prevent it from sticking while it browns. Drain the cooked pasta and return to the pasta pan. Add the bacon bits and any remaining oil from the frying pan.

Add the fromage frais and the pesto sauce and stir carefully until it's all well-mixed.

Reheat gently for a minute and serve with basil leaves

scattered over the top and plenty of freshly ground black pepper.

Serves 4.

PASTA MUSHROOM

Preparation time: 10 minutes
Cooking time: 10-15 minutes

12oz/350g dried pasta
4oz/115g butter, ready-mixed with garlic and herbs
8oz/225g mushrooms, thinly sliced
2oz/55g pinenuts
1 tbsp lemon juice
1 tbsp fresh herbs, chopped
Fresh Parmesan, grated
Freshly ground salt and black pepper

Cook pasta as directed. Five minutes before it is ready, melt the butter and fry the mushrooms for a few minutes or until soft. Add the pinenuts to the pan and stir.

Next, stir in the lemon juice and herbs. Mix well. When the pasta is cooked, drain it well and mix with the mushroom sauce.

Serve at once with the Parmesan, salt and black pepper.

Serves 4.

SMOKED FISH PASTA

Preparation time: 15 minutes
Cooking time: 10-15 minutes

The peas in this recipe can be cooked and drained the night before. Keep them covered and cool. Similarly, the salmon can be cut up and left to soak in the cream and kept covered in the fridge.

12oz/350g dried pasta
4oz/115g smoked salmon, snipped into thin strips
8oz/225g frozen peas, cooked
10 fl oz/300 ml whipping cream
1oz/30g butter
1 tbsp fresh dill, chopped
Fresh Parmesan, grated
Freshly ground salt and black pepper

Cook pasta as directed. Meanwhile, in another pan, melt the butter and add the cooked peas. Toss them gently around to heat through. Add the cream and salmon to the peas and heat gently through. When the pasta is cooked, drain it well and mix with the hot cream and chopped dill. Serve with Parmesan sprinkled over the top and season with salt and black pepper.

Serves 4.

PASTA FETA

Preparation time: 5-10 minutes
Cooking time: 10-15 minutes

12oz/350g dried pasta
10oz/285g Patros Feta cheese cubes in oil and herbs, plus 3 tbsp oil from the jar
8oz/225g thin green beans, topped and tailed and cut into ¹/₂-inch pieces
1 tbsp fresh herbs, chopped such as oregano or chives, or both
Freshly ground salt and black pepper

Cook pasta as directed. Three minutes before the end of the cooking time, add the chopped beans to the pasta water to cook. When the pasta and beans are ready, drain them well and mix carefully with the oil, the cubes of cheese and the herbs.

Put back on the heat for 30 seconds or so, or until the cheese begins to soften. Season to taste.

Serves 4.

Note: this is a good summer pasta to eat outside with a sliced tomato salad and some red wine.

EGG AND CHIVE SPAGHETTI

Preparation time: 5-10 minutes
Cooking time: 10-15 minutes

12oz/350g dried spaghetti
2 large eggs
5 fl oz/150ml single cream
1 large clove garlic, crushed
2 tbsp chives or spring onion tops, chopped
2oz/55g fresh Parmesan, grated
Freshly ground salt and black pepper

Cook the spaghetti as directed. Meanwhile, beat the eggs in a bowl with the crushed garlic, cream, salt and pepper and 1oz/30g of the grated Parmesan. When the spaghetti is cooked, drain it well. Put it back in the pan to heat gently. Add the egg and cream mixture and stir it all round for 30 seconds to a minute — or until the egg starts to set.

Season to taste with the rest of the Parmesan cheese sprinkled over the top.

Serves 4.

ANCHOVY PASTA

Preparation time: 10 minutes
Cooking time: 10-15 minutes

12oz/350g dried pasta
2 tbsp olive oil
3oz/85g anchovies - 1½ tins, plus their oil
2 cloves garlic, crushed
1 tbsp drained, rinsed capers
16 pitted olives, roughly chopped
2 tbsp fresh, chopped herbs such as basil and oregano
Fresh Parmesan, grated
Freshly ground salt and black pepper

Cook pasta as directed. Meanwhile, heat the olive oil in a pan and add the crushed garlic and the anchovies, plus their oil. Stir until the anchovies begin to break up and then add the capers, olives and herbs. When the pasta is cooked and well-drained, mix it carefully with the anchovy sauce. Serve with the Parmesan and season to taste, bearing in mind how salty the anchovies are.

Serves 4.

BUTTERED BROCCOLI PASTA

Preparation time: 10 minutes
Cooking time: 10-15 minutes

12oz/350g dried pasta
8oz/225g broccoli, broken into small florets
4oz/115g butter mixed with herbs and garlic
2oz/55g walnuts, chopped
Freshly ground salt and black pepper

Cook pasta as directed. Three minutes before the end of the cooking time, add the broccoli and continue cooking. When the pasta is ready, drain well, add the butter, mix in the walnuts and heat for a minute. Season and serve.

Serves 4.

Note: if you can't get hold of broccoli, a small bag of frozen peas will do just as well.

MEDITERRANEAN PASTA

Preparation time: 10 minutes
Cooking time: 10-15 minutes

12oz/350g dried pasta
16-20 pitted black olives
2 tbsp capers, drained and rinsed
7oz/200g tinned tuna in oil, drained and flaked
2 cloves garlic, crushed
1 tbsp extra-virgin olive oil
16oz/450g tin chopped tomatoes with herbs
Fresh Parmesan, grated
Freshly ground salt and black pepper

Cook pasta as directed. A couple of minutes before it is ready, heat the oil and add the garlic. Cook for a minute and add the tuna, capers, olives and tomatoes. When the pasta is ready, drain and mix carefully with the tuna sauce. Put it all back on the heat for a minute to gently warm through. Season to taste.

Sprinkle with the Parmesan and serve.

Serves 4.

CREAMY CHICKEN LIVERS

Preparation time: 10 minutes
Cooking time: 5-6 minutes

1lb/450g chicken livers, (if frozen, defrost thoroughly)
2oz/55g butter
1 tbsp olive oil
1 clove garlic, crushed
1 tbsp brandy or dry sherry
1 tbsp French mustard
5 fl oz/150ml double cream
Freshly ground salt and black pepper

Drain the livers, rinse and pat dry. Cut off any sinewy bits and chop into bite-sized pieces. Heat the butter and oil and add the garlic and livers, tossing them quickly around in the pan for two to three minutes.

Now add the brandy or sherry and cook for a further minute before adding the mustard and the cream. Stir and allow to cook for another minute. Season with freshly ground salt and black pepper and serve with rice or noodles.

Serves 3-4.

Note: I find it easier to buy tubs of ready-frozen chicken livers for this recipe. But do remember to take them out of the freezer the night before you need them, to allow them to slowly defrost in the fridge. If you don't like any pink at all in your meat, you may like to cook the livers for a minute or so longer.

LAMB'S LIVER WITH SAGE AND LEMON

Preparation time: 10-15 minutes
Cooking time: 10 minutes

1lb/450g lambs liver, thinly sliced
2oz/55g butter
Juice of ½ lemon
1 clove garlic, chopped
2 tbsp sage leaves, chopped or 1 tsp dried
Freshly ground salt and black pepper

Melt the butter in a frying pan and add the garlic and sage. Cook for 30 seconds. Drop in the liver a few slices at a time. Fry for a couple of minutes on both sides, depending on how pink you like your meat. Add the lemon juice, a little salt and lots of black pepper and serve with new potatoes.

Serves 3-4.

Note: liver is lovely when served extra-thin and this is a fiddly job which needs a sharp knife. So if you have an obliging butcher, ask him to do the honours, or buy it ready sliced from a good supermarket.

MUSHROOM STROGANOFF

Preparation time: 5-10 minutes
Cooking time: 6-7 minutes

12oz/350g button mushrooms, wiped and cut into quarters
2oz/55g butter
3 tbsp dry sherry
½ tsp paprika
7 fl oz/200 ml crème fraîche
2 tbsp lemon juice
1 tbsp parsley, chopped
Freshly ground salt and black pepper

Melt the butter and fry the mushrooms quickly for three minutes. Season with salt, pepper and paprika. Add the sherry and cook for another minute. Stir in crème fraîche. Allow to heat through gently for a further three minutes and then add the lemon juice. Taste before serving, season and add more paprika if needed. Serve at once with noodles or pasta.
Serves 3-4.

TARRAGON AND LEMON CHICKEN

Preparation time: 5 minutes plus marinating time
Cooking time: 25 minutes

4 chicken breasts, skinned
4 tbsp olive oil
2 tbsp lemon juice
1 clove garlic, crushed
2 tbsp chopped fresh tarragon or 1 tsp dried
Freshly ground salt and black pepper

Make a few slits across the top of the chicken breasts. Mix together the oil, lemon juice, garlic and tarragon and pour this over the chicken. Leave to marinate for at least 12 hours, covered, in the fridge. Half an hour before you want to eat, preheat the oven to gas mark 4/180C/350F.
Place the chicken and marinade in an oven-proof dish and grind over a little salt and pepper. Cover and bake for 25 minutes, turning the breasts over halfway through, so they all get a good coating of marinade.
Serves 4.

Note: This dish is best prepared the night before to allow the chicken to marinate properly.

PEPPER AND JUNIPER STEAK

Preparation time: 15 minutes plus marinating time
Cooking time: 10 minutes

Another dish which is the better for preparing the night before.

1lb/450g sirloin steak, sliced into thin strips
1 tbsp Worcestershire sauce
1 tbsp soy sauce
2 tsp runny honey
1 clove garlic, crushed
1 tbsp juniper berries, crushed
1 tbsp olive oil
Freshly ground salt and black pepper

Make a marinade by mixing the Worcestershire sauce, soy sauce, honey, garlic and juniper berries. Place the steak strips in a dish and pour over the marinade. Leave for at least a couple of hours, covered, in the fridge, or overnight if at all possible. When ready to cook, heat the oil in a frying pan. Drain the steak from the marinade with a slotted spoon and fry quickly in the oil for five minutes to brown. Next, add what's left of the marinade and cook for a further five minutes over a slightly gentler heat.

Add salt and black pepper to taste and serve with pasta or noodles.

Serves 4.

SPICED PORK

Preparation time: 10 minutes
Cooking time: 10 minutes

1lb/450g pork escalopes, (about 8)
7oz/200ml natural yoghurt
1 tbsp curry paste
2 tbsp mango chutney
1 tbsp fresh coriander, chopped
1 tbsp fresh ginger, grated
Freshly ground salt and black pepper

Mix together the yoghurt, curry paste, mango chutney, coriander and ginger and coat the steaks in this mixture. Leave to marinate for a few hours, or overnight, covered, in the fridge.

When ready to eat, heat up a non-stick frying pan and cook the marinated steaks for three minutes on each side. Serve with rice or pasta and salad. A squeeze of lemon or lime goes well over the top of this dish.

Note: Again, it is best to prepare this dish the night before. Serves 4.

CHICKEN IN GARLIC CREAM

Preparation time: 5-10 minutes
Cooking time: 15-20 minutes

4 x 6oz/170g chicken breasts, skinned
1oz/30g butter
1 tbsp olive oil
1 small onion, grated
3 cloves garlic, crushed
7 fl oz/200ml double cream
1 bay leaf
1 tbsp fresh parsley, chopped
Freshly ground salt and black pepper

Heat the butter and the oil and cook the onion for a couple of minutes or until soft. Stir with a spoon while frying to stop it burning. Add the cream, garlic and bayleaf, season with the salt and pepper and heat until the cream is just boiling. Add the chicken breasts, trying to get them all in the pan in one layer.

Put a lid on the pan, turn down the heat and simmer gently for 12-15 minutes, turning the chicken halfway through the cooking time.

Serve with parsley sprinkled over the top. This is very rich, so eat it with plain rice or boiled potatoes.

Serves 4.

WHITING IN A MUSTARD SAUCE

Preparation time: 5-10 minutes
Cooking time: 15 minutes

4 pieces of whiting, each approx 5oz/140g
1oz/30g butter
1 tbsp coarse grain mustard
4 tbsp crème fraîche
1 tbsp gherkins, chopped
Freshly ground salt and black pepper

Preheat the oven to gas mark 7/220C/425F. Grease a large shallow ovenproof dish and arrange the fillets in it, trying not to overlap them. Season them lightly with a little salt and pepper.

Meanwhile, mix the crème fraîche with the mustard and gherkins. Spoon this mixture evenly over the fish and cook, uncovered, for 15 minutes.

Serves 4.

Note: you can use other flat, white fish here too.

GINGERED SCALLOPS

Preparation time: 10 minutes
Cooking time: 5-8 minutes

1lb/450g scallops (if king scallops, slice in half; if queenies, leave whole)
1 head chinese cabbage, thinly sliced
2 tbsp sesame oil
1 tbsp dark soy sauce
6 spring onions, snipped
1 clove garlic, crushed
2 tsp fresh ginger, grated
Freshly ground salt and black pepper

Heat the sesame oil in a large frying pan until it's very hot. Add the chinese cabbage, spring onions, garlic and ginger and stir quickly for two to three minutes, or until the leaves are starting to wilt.

Next add the scallops and soy sauce and heat for a further couple of minutes, making sure that they get cooked through evenly.

Adjust seasoning and serve at once.

Serves 4.

Note: Frozen scallops which might be slightly lacking in taste do very well in this dish, but make sure that you take them out of the freezer to defrost before you leave for work.

PESTO TUNA

Preparation time: 5 minutes
Cooking time 10 minutes

The marinade can be prepared in advance. Keep it in a jar in the fridge. The tuna steaks will marinate quite happily all day in the fridge — then when you come home, all you have to do is grill them.

4 tuna steaks, approx 6 oz/170g each
4 tbsp olive oil
3 tbsp pesto sauce
2 tbsp lemon juice
Freshly ground black pepper

Put the fish in a shallow, heatproof dish. For the marinade, mix the oil, pesto, lemon juice and pepper. Spoon this over the fish and leave for at least half an hour.

When ready to eat, turn the grill on to high and cook the fish for five minutes on one side, making sure there's lots of marinade over it. Then turn the fish over and grill the other side for a further five minutes, again basting as you go.

Serve with boiled or baked potatoes.

Serves 4.

Note: this is a good way of pepping up any frozen white fish that might otherwise be lacking in taste.

SALMON WITH SPINACH AND MINT

Preparation time: 10 minutes
Cooking time: 7-10 minutes

4 salmon steaks, about 6oz/170g and ¹/₂ inch/13mm thick.
4oz/115g fresh young spinach leaves
2 tbsp fresh mint, chopped
1 lemon, sliced
2oz/55g butter
Freshly ground salt and black pepper

Preheat oven to gas mark 7/220C/425F. Roughly chop the spinach leaves and mix with the chopped mint. A food processor does it beautifully and will save time.

Take four sheets of foil, each one big enough to cover each fish. Divide the spinach and mint into eight portions. Put one portion on each of the four sheets of foil. Top that with a salmon steak, seasoned with salt and black pepper.

Spread the remaining spinach and mint over the top of the steaks. Then top each one with half an ounce of butter and a lemon slice. Now squeeze any remaining juice from the lemon over the fish and bring the edges of the foil together to make four parcels. They should be tightly sealed while not actually touching the fish.

Cook in the preheated oven for seven to ten minutes. Check them after seven minutes. If the steaks are thick, they may need a couple of minutes longer.

Serves 4.

Note: if you haven't got fresh, use frozen spinach, but ensure that it's thawed and well-squeezed, to get rid of excess water.

CHICKEN IN LEMON

Preparation time: 10-15 minutes
Cooking time: 10 minutes

1lb/450g chicken, cut into strips
5 fl oz/150ml chicken stock
Grated rind and juice of ½ lemon
1 tbsp fresh thyme leaves, chopped or 1 level tsp dried
14oz/400g fromage frais
Freshly ground salt and black pepper

Add the thyme, lemon rind and juice to the chicken stock and bring to the boil in a pan. Next, put in the chicken strips and poach for five minutes. Remove the chicken with a slotted draining spoon and keep warm.

Turn up the heat and quickly reduce the chicken stock until there is a third left. Stir in the fromage frais. Taste and season and add the warm, cooked chicken strips. Eat with noodles.

Serves 4.

CARROTY BEEFBURGERS

Preparation time: 15 minutes
Cooking time: 25 minutes

This dish is best suited to preparing the night before and keeping in the fridge.

1lb/450g minced beef
2 medium sized carrots, approx 6oz/170g, peeled and grated
1 small onion, grated, or the green tops, snipped from 4 spring onions
1 tbsp parsley, chopped
1 egg, beaten
1 tbsp olive oil
Freshly ground salt and black pepper

Mix everything together — I like to add a good ½ tsp of salt but you may like to add less.

Shape into approximately eight beefburgers. If making this in advance, put them on a plate and leave, covered, in the fridge.

When ready to eat, heat the oven to gas mark 5/190C/375F. Grease an ovenproof tray and place the beefburgers on it, a couple of inches apart. Drizzle the oil evenly over the tops of them and cook for 20-25 minutes.

Serves 4.

Note: this is delicious with a yoghurt and cucumber sauce. Simply grate a couple of inches of cucumber into a small pot of natural yoghurt and you have your sauce.

CHERVILLED TURKEY

Preparation time: 5 minutes
Cooking time: 15 minutes

4 turkey escalopes, each about 4oz/115g
2oz/55g butter
8 tbsp crème fraîche
1 tbsp fresh chervil, chopped
Freshly ground salt and black pepper

Preheat oven to gas mark 5/190C/375F. Butter a shallow ovenproof dish. Melt the butter in a frying pan and gently fry the turkey escalopes for a minute on each side or until golden-brown. As they cook, season them with salt and pepper. Remove the turkey from the pan and put it in the ovenproof dish.

Put the pan back on the heat and add the crème fraîche. Stir it around, scraping the bottom to get all the buttery flavours. Mix in the chervil and pour the sauce over the turkey. Pop the dish in the oven and cook, uncovered, for 12 minutes.

Serves 4.

Note: this can also be made with other herbs — such as chopped tarragon or parsley.

Chicken with Anchovy and Thyme

Preparation time: 10 minutes
Cooking time: 20 minutes

4 chicken breasts, each cut into quarters
2 tbsp olive oil
1 clove garlic, crushed
A handful of fresh thyme leaves or 1 tsp dried
6 anchovy fillets
5 fl oz/150ml dry white wine
2 medium tomatoes, chopped roughly
Freshly ground salt and black pepper

Heat the oil in a frying pan and add the chicken bits. Brown them quickly on all sides. Add the wine, thyme, garlic, anchovies and black pepper. (Go easy on the salt since the anchovies are salty!) Bring it all to the boil.

Reduce the heat, cover and cook gently for 10 minutes. Then, add the chopped tomatoes and cook uncovered for another five minutes. Adjust seasoning and serve.

Serves 4.

Chicken in Red Pesto Sauce

Preparation time: 5 minutes
Cooking time: 20 minutes

This is better left to marinate overnight before you cook it. Or better still, cook it and serve cold the next day. It's really delicious!

4 chicken breasts, each cut into quarters
1 tbsp olive oil
5 fl oz/150ml crème fraîche
2 tbsp red pesto sauce
8oz/225g tomatoes, roughly chopped
12 black olives, pitted and left whole
1 tsp lemon juice
Freshly ground salt and black pepper

Heat the oil in a frying pan and quickly brown the chicken breast pieces. Meanwhile, mix the crème fraîche, the red pesto and the tomatoes in a bowl. Pour this mixture over the chicken pieces and stir carefully whilst bringing to the boil. Cover and cook gently for 15 minutes. Adjust seasoning at the end and add the olives.

Serve with plain pasta or new potatoes and a salad.

Serves 4.

Note: this is also good made with tinned tomatoes. Use a 16oz/450g tin of chopped tomatoes, drained of their juice.

LEEK CROUSTADE

Preparation time for the base: 10 minutes, less with a food processor.
Cooking time: 12-15 minutes

You can make the base the night before and keep it in the fridge.

For the base:

6oz/170g fresh breadcrumbs (brown is best)
2oz/55g butter or margarine
4oz/115g Cheddar cheese, grated
4oz/115g chopped nuts (buy them ready-chopped in a bag)
½ tsp dried mixed herbs
2 cloves garlic, crushed
2 tbsp fresh parsley, chopped

Preheat oven to gas mark 6/200C/400F. Butter a 9in/23cm flan dish. Rub the breadcrumbs and butter together until you have fine crumbs. Alternatively put them in the food processor and whizz until ready. Next add the cheese, nuts, herbs, garlic and parsley and mix around. Press this mixture into the base of the flan dish.

Bake for 12-15 minutes in the oven, until slightly browned and firm.

Preparation time for topping: 10 minutes
Cooking time: 20 minutes

For the topping:

4 medium leeks, trimmed, cleaned and finely chopped
7oz/200g tin chopped tomatoes, drained of their juice
3 tbsp olive oil
5 fl oz/150ml crème fraîche
1oz/30g Gruyère cheese, grated
Freshly ground salt and pepper

Preheat oven to gas mark 6/200C/400F. Heat oil in a saucepan, add the leeks and fry for a couple of minutes. Add the drained tomatoes and cook for a further few minutes with a lid on, until the leeks are tender. Season with salt and pepper. Add crème fraîche and mix well. Pour the mixture over the base you have already made. Sprinkle the Gruyère cheese over the top and bake for 15 minutes or until the top is browned and bubbly.

Serves 4-6

Note: this may seem a complicated recipe, but it is really quite simple and is absolutely delicious. Eat with a green salad and, since it's quite filling, I suggest very little else. This is from my good friend, Giselle Hammond; the best cook I know north of the Border, but then she is French!

CORNED BEEF PIE

Preparation time: 10-15 minutes
Cooking time: 20 minutes

1 x 10in/25cm cooked, plain pastry case
3 tbsp spring onion tops, snipped
7oz/200g tin corned beef, roughly chopped
8oz/225g mashed potato
1 tbsp Worcestershire sauce
2oz/55g Cheddar cheese, grated
Freshly ground salt and black pepper

Preheat oven to gas mark 4/180C/350F. Mix together the onion, potato, corned beef, Worcestershire sauce and seasoning. Spoon into the pastry case and level out. Sprinkle the cheese evenly over the top and put in the oven for 20 minutes to heat through.

Serves 4

TUNA AND SWEETCORN FLAN

Preparation time: 10 minutes
Cooking time: 20 minutes

1 x 10in/25cm cooked plain pastry case
7oz/200g tinned tuna, drained and flaked
7oz/200g tin sweetcorn, drained
6oz/170g small tin Carnation milk
1 egg, beaten
4oz/115g cheese, grated — any leftover hard cheese will
  do
Freshly ground salt and black pepper

Heat oven to gas mark 4/180C/350F. Mix together the tuna, sweetcorn, milk, cheese and egg. Season with salt and pepper. Spoon into the flan and cook for 20-25 minutes or until set.

Serves 4.

LAINEY'S STILTON WHISKY MUSHROOMS IN A CASE

Preparation time: 10 minutes
Cooking time: 10 minutes

12oz/350g small button mushrooms, wiped
2oz/55g butter
1 onion, grated
4oz/115g Stilton cheese, crumbled
3 tbsp Scotch whisky
4 tbsp double cream
1 x 10in/25cm cooked plain pastry case (I like to use
  wholemeal)
Parsley, chopped to garnish
Freshly ground salt and black pepper

Heat the oven to gas mark 2/150C/300F and put in the flan case to heat through. Melt the butter in a frying pan and fry the onion for a minute, stirring around so that it doesn't burn. Next, add the mushrooms to the pan and cook for three to four minutes, ensuring that they they all get a coating of butter. Add the whisky, cheese and the cream and heat gently until the cheese is melted. Add pepper, but taste before adding salt, since the Stilton is already salty. Take the pastry case from the oven and fill with the mushroom mixture. Sprinkle parsley over the top for colour and serve.

Serves 4.

Note: this recipe is from my friend Elaine Mallinson. She usually puts the sauce into a puff pastry case and you may like to do the same or use large, cooked vol-au-vent cases and serve these as a starter. I have used the plain pastry case simply for extra convenience.

TOMATO TART

Preparation time: 10 minutes
Cooking time: 12-15 minutes

4 x 5in/13cm ready-rolled puff pastry squares
12oz/350g tomatoes, sliced
2 tbsp tapenade (olive paste)
1 tbsp olive oil
A handful of pitted olives, chopped
A handful of basil leaves, chopped
Salt and freshly milled black pepper.

Preheat oven to gas mark 7/220C/425F. Grease a baking sheet and put it in the oven to heat. Spread half a tablespoon of tapenade over each pastry sheet and top that with the sliced tomatoes, dividing them out evenly between the sheets. Next, brush the tomatoes with olive oil. Grind on salt and pepper and sprinkle with the olives and basil.

Take the baking sheet from the oven and with a couple of fish slices, carefully lift the pastry squares onto the baking sheet. Bake for 15 minutes at the top of the oven and serve with lots of black pepper.

Serves 4.

Note: if you can't get ready-rolled puff pastry squares, buy an 8oz/230g pack and roll that out into an oblong shape and make one large tart instead.

Home and Dry...

...I DON'T MIND COMMUTING. I USE THE JOURNEY TO PLAN WHAT
I'M GOING TO DO AND THE RETURN TRIP TO WORK OUT WHY I
DIDN'T GET IT DONE.

(New York commuter)

Well, you're nearly there! Now for the puddings and I am a great believer in fresh fruit which make delicious and simple dishes, either served on its own or spiced up a little.

For example, take a ripe **pineapple,** peel, slice and serve with a splash of cherry brandy or amaretto; halve a juicy **melon,** deseed and fill with fresh raspberries; peel a juicy pear, slice and eat with a tablespoon of fruity fromage frais.

Fresh **figs** are wonderful and there's a certain time of year when the city barrow boys sell off trays of them really cheaply. Buy a dozen or so, try not to devour them before you get home, and serve for dessert with some lovely, creamy Brie.

A **peach** or a **nectarine** served with a ripe blue-veined cheese is out of this world, but my own favourite has to be a crunchy **Granny Smith's apple** and a chunk of Lancashire creamy cheese. If you're ever passing through Preston, do buy some of this delicious cheese, because it freezes well and tastes like heaven.

When the **strawberry** season arrives, serve them just as they come, or mix with whipped cream and crushed meringues to make a delicious fruit pudding. Instead of strawberries, substitute with **raspberries** or **bananas** and perhaps a splash of fruit liqueur too.

Fresh is definitely best when it comes to fruit, but tinned or bottled varieties can be a great help to the commuting cook. Do try to buy produce canned in fruit juice rather than syrup. The exception to this are **black cherries** in syrup, which are wonderful heated gently through and served with ice cream.

Things like tinned **peaches** and **apricots** are handy because they provide a good base for a fruit crumble. Tinned **blackcurrants** are also useful to have in; drained and mixed into creamy Greek yoghurt, they are an ideal end to a meal.

As for frozen fruit, raspberries don't come to much harm in the freezer and blackcurrants fare very well indeed. So, if you've a summer glut of either, it's worth putting some away for the winter. Try to freeze them on trays so that they can be transferred into a freezer bag individually when frozen. This way they will defrost better and not thaw out into one large, mushy lump.

On the subject of fruit, I can thoroughly recommend a French **compote** called Bonne Maman. It consists of whole fruit cooked in a light syrup and comes in a variety of flavours and is really wonderful for mixing with cream or putting on pancakes, puff pastry or simply eating on its own.

Fruit apart, I always try to keep a good quality **ice-cream** in the freezer, because that's the easiest pudding standby of all. I've yet to meet a person who doesn't like ice-cream and some of the flavours you can buy these days are extraordinarily varied.

And if you've got ice-cream, you may like to keep some **chocolate** in the cupboard. For example, a Mars bar, chopped up and melted into a couple of tablespoons of cream makes a scrumptious sauce for ice-cream.

Honey goes well with ice-cream too. Melt four tablespoons of honey with a couple of ounces of butter and a handful of nuts for a wonderful taste with a lovely contrast between hot and cold. Or, for another simple but delicious dessert, drizzle some runny honey over creamy Greek yoghurt and top with a few toasted nuts.

Meanwhile, a few thoughts on **cream.** Whipping it does take time — but the job can be made easier with a small electric whisk. You can whip it up the night before and keep it covered in a bowl in the fridge, or whip it a few days before and put it in the freezer. Runny cream does not freeze well, but once it's whipped up and well-covered, I've discovered that it will keep for a couple of weeks in the freezer. So, take it out of the freezer in the morning before you go to work, pop it into the fridge and when you come back at night, your cream will be waiting, ready-whipped and ready to use!

And finally on the subject of cream: I seem to have used a lot of it in these recipes, but you can substitute **Greek yoghurt** in some of them if you are really worried about calories. Another alternative is to use **crème fraîche**, which does not need whipping and also has a longer shelf-life than cream.

COLD PUDDINGS

MACAROON CUSTARD

Preparation time: 10 minutes if using bought custard
Cooking time: none

This should be made in advance and kept covered in the fridge.

18 medium (1 inch) amaretto or macaroon biscuits
3 tbsp brandy, amaretto or orange juice
1 pt/575ml carton good-quality custard
3 chocolate Flake bars

Arrange the biscuits in a pretty glass dish and evenly sprinkle over the alcohol or fruit juice. Crumble two of the Flakes over the top of that. Pour over the custard. You can make your own, but some of the ready-made ones are very good (especially M&S!)
Sprinkle another Flake on top and serve.
Serves 4.
Note: I've tried this using chocolate-chip biscuits instead of macaroons and it's equally delicious!

GINGER KIWIS

Preparation time: 10-15 minutes
Cooking time: a few minutes to brown the nuts.

6 ripe Kiwi fruits
2oz/55g pine nuts
4 tbsp orange juice
7oz/200g Greek yoghurt
½ inch stem ginger, from a jar, finely chopped, plus 1
tbsp syrup from the jar

Toast the nuts under the grill until lightly browned or dry-fry them in a frying pan. Allow to cool. Peel and slice the fruit and put it in a dish. Spoon the orange juice and the stem ginger syrup evenly over this and then sprinkle the nuts on top.

Mix the chopped ginger with the yoghurt and serve as a sauce for the Kiwi fruits.

Serves 4.

Note: this is a fairly tangy dessert. If you like something a little sweeter, add a tablespoon of runny honey to sweeten the yoghurt. It is also possible to buy nuts ready-toasted, which is a boon for the hard-pressed cook!

TWO-BERRY MARY

Preparation time: 5-10 minutes, depending on whether you have a food processor
Cooking time: none

The raspberry sauce can be made the night before and kept in a jar in the fridge.

1lb/450g strawberries
8oz/225g raspberries
2oz/55g icing sugar

Wash and hull the strawberries and place them in a glass dish. If you have a processor, whizz the raspberries and sugar until you have a purée. If not, press the raspberries through a sieve and mix the sugar in by hand. Spoon the raspberry purée over the strawberries and serve.

Serves 4.

Note: you can make this with other fruits, for example, puréed blackcurrants sweetened with icing sugar and spooned over fresh blackberries. If the purée seems a little thick, thin it with a spoonful of apple juice.

HADRIAN'S WALL CHOCOLATE PUDDING

Preparation time: 15-20 minutes (less if cream is ready-whipped)
Cooking time: none

This is best made the night before and kept covered in the fridge.

3 flat tbsp cocoa chocolate
1 flat tbsp drinking chocolate
1 flat tbsp coffee powder (not granules)
4oz/115g real breadcrumbs
2 heaped tbsp demerara sugar
1 pint/575ml whipping cream

Mix together the cocoa, drinking chocolate, coffee powder, breadcrumbs and sugar. Whip the cream until firm. Starting with the chocolate, spread alternating layers of cream and chocolate in a glass dish. Finish with a layer of chocolate.

Leave overnight before serving.

Serves 4-6.

Note: this is a lovely, simple pudding from home territory, given to me by my friend Madge who lives on Hadrian's Wall. The original recipe only used drinking chocolate, but I have added cocoa to make it less sweet. Madge says it's not her own recipe, so credit due to whoever is responsible!

HONEYED CURRANTS

Preparation time: 5-10 minutes, depending on how long it takes to hull the fruit
Cooking time: none

This improves by letting it keep a while.

1lb/450g blackcurrants, washed and hulled
6 tbsp runny honey
4 tbsp crème de cassis

Destalk currants and place in a dish. Pour over the honey, followed by the crème de cassis. When ready to serve, mix it all together gently and eat with crème fraîche or yoghurt.

Serves 4.

Note: this is lovely made with redcurrants too.

CRUNCHY LEMON SYLLABUB

Preparation time: 10 minutes
Cooking time: none

This can be partially prepared the night before, but do not

add the biscuit crumbs until ready to eat, otherwise the pudding will lose its 'crunch'!

10 fl oz/300 ml crème fraîche
Finely grated rind and juice of 1 lemon
12 macaroon biscuits
4oz/115g caster sugar

Crumble the macaroon biscuits finely. I put mine into a bag and bash them with a rolling pin! Mix together the sugar and crème fraîche. Add the lemon juice and rind and mix in the biscuit crumbs. Divide the mixture between four sundae glasses.
Serves 4.

PEACHES IN WHITE WINE

Preparation time: 10 minutes
Cooking time: none

Make this several hours in advance and keep it covered and cool.

6 ripe peaches
3 tbsp caster sugar
Finely grated rind of 1 lemon
10 fl oz/300ml dry, white wine

Skin the peaches by dipping them, one by one, into a bowl of boiling water for 10-15 seconds and then plunge them into cold water. The skins should peel off easily, but don't let them steep for too long in the hot water since the flesh will mush!
Once peeled, cut them into quarters, remove the stones and pop them in a dish. Sprinkle with the sugar, pour the wine around the peices and leave to soak for at least 30 minutes.
Serves 4.
Note: If you've a particularly sweet tooth, then you might like to use sweet dessert wine instead, but don't use 10 fl oz, unless you want to end up on the floor! Peel, stone and cut your fruit as above and divide it between the four sundae glasses. Spoon a little dessert wine into each glass and leave the peach quarters to soak for twenty minutes or so. Eat with some crispy, sweet biscuits and imagine you're in heaven ...

CRUNCHIE ICE-CREAM

Preparation time: 10 minutes
Cooking time: none
Freezing time: at least half an hour

1 small block/35 fl oz or 1½ pints/1 litre soft-serve ice-cream
4 Crunchie bars

Take the ice-cream out of the freezer for a few minutes to allow it to soften a little more. Keeping the Crunchie bars in their wrappers, bash them with a rolling pin until you have reduced them to crumbs. Mix the Crunchie crumbs into the ice-cream and refreeze until needed.
Serves 4.

FRUITY MERINGUE CREAMS

Preparation time: 10-15 minutes (less if cream is ready-whipped)
Cooking time: none

10oz/285g Bonne Maman cherry compote from a jar
4 medium-sized meringues
2oz/55g caster sugar
5 fl oz/150 ml double cream

Put the cream in a good-sized mixing bowl and whip it until firm but not stiff. With your hands, break the meringues into the cream mixture — you want them in bite-sized pieces. Mix it all gently around and then stir in the sugar. Take four sundae glasses or small glass bowls and put a tablespoon of the cherry compote into the bottom of each glass. Follow that with a dollop of meringue cream.
Alternate with cherries and meringue. Finish with the cream, and a bit of cherry swirled in the middle. Eat within the hour.
Serves 4.
Note: this can also be made with fruits of the forest, which come in handy one-pint cartons and can be bought at good supermarkets.

LYNNIE'S SUMMER FRUITS IN RED WINE

Preparation time: 10 minutes
Cooking time: none

This is best made well in advance and left for a couple of days.

1 lb/450g mixed summer fruits — strawberries, raspberries, blueberries etc.
Around three-quarters a bottle of light, fruity, red wine
Caster sugar to taste

Prepare by washing the fruit and put it in a non-metallic dish. Sprinkle over 2 tbsp sugar, or more if the fruit is a little sour. Pour over the red wine, cover and store in the fridge, stirring occasionally.

Taste and add more sugar if required. It takes a couple of days for the flavour to mature.

Serves 4.

Note: This is terribly easy to make, but you should prepare it well in advance. If you can make it on Thursday for a dinner party on Saturday, then that would be ideal. It must, though, be kept cool, otherwise it will start to ferment. Serve with crème fraîche and brandy-snap biscuits.

MANGO AND LIME WHIP

Preparation time: 5-10 minutes
Cooking time: none

This is good made the night before and kept covered in the fridge.

1lb/450g tinned mango slices, drained
7 fl oz/200 ml crème fraîche
Juice of half a lime

Purée the fruit in a food processor or press it through a sieve. Combine the purée with the crème fraîche and lime juice and spoon into individual glasses. If time permits, grate over a little lime peel when ready to serve.

Serves 4.

Note: tinned peaches or pears also make a delicious whip. For more texture, do not puree the fruit, but mash with a fork.

BOOZY CHOCOLATE CREAM

Preparation time: 10 minutes
Cooking time: none

4 Crunchie bars
10 fl oz/300 ml double cream
2 tbsp chocolate liqueur

Crush the Crunchie bars by keeping them sealed in their wrappers and bashing them with a rolling pin until they're in crumbs. Whip the cream until it's firm. Fold the Crunchie bits into the cream, mix in the chocolate liqueur and divide between four sundae glasses.
Serves 4.

RASPBERRY BRULÉE

Preparation time: 5-10 minutes
Cooking time: 2-3 minutes

This is best made in advance and kept covered and cool.

1lb/450g raspberries
14oz/400g Greek yoghurt
4 tbsp soft brown sugar

Turn the grill to its highest setting. Butter a shallow, heat-proof dish, put in the fruit and spoon over the yoghurt. Sprinkle the sugar evenly over the top and then pop it all under the grill. Wait until the sugar melts, but watch it carefully, because it may only take a minute or so.
Allow to cool before serving.
Serves 4.
Note: with luck, your raspberries will be ripe and sweet, but if not, you can always sprinkle over a tablespoon of caster sugar before adding the yoghurt. This pudding is delicious made with other soft fruit such as peaches or strawberries. However, if it's getting near the end of the week and you've run out of anything fresh, then a large tin of blackcurrants or apricots will make a respectable second best, but don't forget to drain them first.

GINGER SNAP DELIGHT

Preparation time: 15 minutes (less if cream is ready-whipped)
Cooking time: none

This can be made the night before and kept, covered, in the fridge.

One packet of ginger biscuits (around 30)
10 fl oz/300ml double cream
4 tbsp brandy
Something for decoration — a couple of pieces of chopped stem ginger, or a sliced Kiwi fruit

Whip the cream until it is nice and thick. Put the brandy in a saucer and dip the biscuits quickly into it on both sides. Next place a layer of the soused biscuits at the bottom of a shallow dish. Spread a quarter of the cream over the biscuits and then place another layer of biscuits on top of that. Continue with cream and biscuits until they're all used up.

Decorate with chopped stem ginger or fruit and leave for couple of hours before eating.

Serves 4.

Note: this will taste the better for being made in advance. Tee-totallers can use the juice from a can of peaches for soaking the biscuits and use the fruit for decoration.

BANANAS AMARETTO

Preparation time: 10 minutes
Cooking time: none

2 large, ripe bananas, thinly sliced
16 x 1 inch amaretto biscuits, crushed into crumbs
2 tbsp amaretto liqueur
10 fl oz/300ml whipping cream

Whip cream until firm but not stiff. In four sundae glasses, layer bananas, cream, biscuit crumbs and amaretto, finishing with the crumbs.

Serves 4.

PORT BERRY CREAM

Preparation time: 15 minutes (less if cream is ready-whipped)
Cooking time: none

Part of this recipe can be made in advance

10 fl oz/300 ml double cream
1lb/450g strawberries, halved if small, quartered if large
2 tbsp port
2oz/55g icing sugar
A few mint leaves, chopped finely

Whip the cream until it stands in soft peaks. Mix it with the port. Sieve the icing sugar into the cream mixture and mix gently around. This part can be made the night before and left covered in the fridge.

When ready to serve, gently mix in the mint leaves and the fruit, reserving eight halves of strawberry for decoration. Divide between four glasses and decorate with the remaining strawberries.

Serves 4.

HOT PUDDINGS

PEARS IN HONEY

Preparation time: 10-15 minutes
Cooking time: 25-30 minutes

8 small, firm pears
4 heaped tbsp runny honey
1 level tsp cinnamon

Preheat the oven to gas mark 4/180C/350F. Peel the pears and put whole, into an ovenproof dish. Spoon over the honey and sprinkle the cinnamon evenly over the top. Cover and cook for 25-30 minutes, turning once halfway through the cooking time, so everything gets covered in honey. You'll know when they are ready since they should be soft but not soggy.

Eat with cream or custard.

Serves 4.

PEACHES IN FRESH ORANGE

Preparation time: 10 minutes
Cooking time: 20 minutes

4 ripe but firm peaches
10 fl oz/300 ml orange juice
7 fl oz/200 ml crème fraîche

Preheat oven to gas mark 4/180C/350F. Skin the peaches by dipping them one by one in a bowl of boiling water for 10-15 seconds and then plunging them into cold water. Halve the fruit and gently remove the stones. Pop the halves in a buttered ovenproof dish and pour the orange juice over.

Cook in a medium oven for 20 minutes, turning them over halfway through the cooking time. Leave to cool slightly and eat with the crème fraîche.

Serves 4.

HOT BUTTERY BANANAS

Preparation and cooking time: 5-10 minutes

4 bananas
2oz/55g butter
2oz/55g soft dark brown sugar
1 tbsp brandy or, if preferred, apple juice

Melt the butter in a frying pan. Peel the bananas and add them whole to the pan. Fry the bananas gently for a couple of minutes, turning them so they all get a covering of butter. Sprinkle with the sugar, juice or brandy, whichever is preferred.

Eat at once with ice-cream or cream.

Serves 4.

HOT BRANDIED APPLES

Preparation time: 10 minutes
Cooking time: 6-7 minutes

2oz/55g butter
3 dessert apples, cored, sliced, but not peeled
2 tsp icing sugar
2 tbsp chopped walnuts
7 fl oz/200 ml crème fraîche
1 tbsp brandy

Heat the butter in the pan and fry the apple rings gently until tender. Pop them into a shallow dish and sprinkle with the icing sugar and nuts. Mix the brandy into the crème fraîche and spoon it all over the top of the apples. Eat it at once, before it melts!

Serves 4.

CHERRY CUSTARD

Preparation time: 15 minutes
Cooking time: 30-40 minutes

This takes a while to cook, but I've included it because it's so easy to prepare and can be eaten cold the next day.

1lb/450g fresh cherries, washed and destalked
4 eggs
10 fl oz/300 ml milk
5 fl oz/150 ml cream
3 oz/80g caster sugar
Several drops almond essence

Heat oven to gas mark 4/180F/350C. Butter a 1½ pint, oval ovenproof dish. Put the cherries in a layer at the bottom of the dish. Beat together the eggs, sugar, essence, milk and cream. Pour this over the cherries and bake, uncovered in the oven for 30-40 minutes, or until the custard is set. Serve warm or cold.

Serves 4-6

Note: if you can't get fresh cherries, a 1lb tin of cherries, drained of their syrup, will come in very useful here!

HOT BUTTERED PLUMS

Taken from *Real Fast Food* by Nigel Slater (I have added the cinnamon!)

Preparation time: 15 minutes
Cooking time: 15-20 minutes

4 slices white bread
2oz/55g butter
8 ripe, sweet plums, halved and stoned
8 tbsp demerara sugar
¹/₂ tsp cinnamon

Preheat oven to gas mark 6/200C/400F. Cut the crusts off the bread and butter each slice thickly, leaving a tiny bit, a teaspoon or so for the top. Lay the bread, not overlapping, in a buttered shallow dish and sprinkle over 6 tbsp of the sugar.

Place the plums, flat side up, on the bread. Dot over a few specks of the remaining butter and sprinkle over the last of the sugar and the cinnamon. Bake in the oven for 15-20 minutes until the butter has melted and the plum juices are bubbling.

Serve hot with custard.

Serves 4.

STUFFED BAKED PEACHES

Preparation time: 15 minutes
Cooking time: 15 minutes

4 firm, ripe peaches
8 x 1 inch/25cm macaroon biscuits
A few drops almond essence
2 tbsp jam — apricot or raspberry
2oz/55g flaked almonds

Preheat oven to gas mark 5/190C/375F. Skin the peaches by dipping them, one by one, into boiling water for 10-15 seconds and then plunge them into cold water. The skins should slip off. Halve each peach and carefully remove the stone.

Crumble the macaroon biscuits and mix with the jam and the essence. Fill the peach halves with the crumb mixture, dividing it evenly. Place the fruit, flat side up, in a buttered heatproof dish, sprinkle with the almonds and bake for 15

minutes in the oven. Eat with Greek yoghurt.
Serves 4.
Note: this dish is equally good made with ripe nectarines.

JUBILEE CHERRIES

Preparation time: 5-10 minutes
Cooking time: 5 minutes

16oz/440g canned black cherries in syrup
4 tbsp redcurrant jelly
Juice and rind of 1 orange
2 tbsp amaretto

Drain the cherries and put in a pan. Add redcurrant jelly
and orange juice and rind and liqueur. Stir over a gentle heat
until the jelly has dissolved and the cherries are warmed
through. Eat with ice-cream or crème fraîche.
Serves 3-4
Note: if you're lucky enough to have fresh cherries, use
those!

FRUIT CRUMBLE

Yes, believe it or not, a crumble is a doddle to make, especially if you have a processor. Commuting cooks without one
can always cheat and buy a good quality packet of crumble
mix...

Preparation time: 10 minutes
Cooking time: 25 minutes

The crumble topping can be made the night before and
kept, covered, in a cool place — but not the fridge since it
tends to go cloggy. The fruit can also be prepared the night
before and kept covered. Then all you have to do when you
come in from work is to put the two together...

1lb/450g soft fruit — blackberries, gooseberries, rasp-
berries, hulled and washed
6oz/85g plain four
3oz/85g butter
6oz/170g caster sugar

Preheat oven to gas mark 5/190C/375F. Put the flour in the food processor with the butter. Process for a few seconds until it turns into fine crumbs. Put it into another bowl and mix in 3oz/85g of the sugar. Butter a deep-sided dish and put in the fruit. Sprinkle over the remaining 3oz/85g sugar.

Cover the fruit with the crumble mixture and bake in the oven for 25 minutes, or until it's nicely browned on top.

Serve warm with cream or crème fraîche.

Serves 4.

Note: don't forget that things like your tinned blackcurrants will come in very useful here if you are out of fresh fruit. Also remember that while some fruits, such as peaches, will not need as much sugar as I've suggested, others, like goose-berries, will need more.

RAISIN FRITTERS

Preparation time: 15 minutes
Cooking time: a few minutes

The batter can be made the night before and kept, cov-ered, in the fridge.

For the batter:

2oz/55g plain flour
1oz/30g ground almonds
2 eggs
5 tbsp double cream
4oz/115g raisins
2oz/55g caster sugar
Grated peel of 1 orange (keep the orange to serve with)

To fry:

1oz/30g butter
1 tbsp vegetable oil

Finely grate the peel from the orange. Put the flour, ground almonds and grated orange peel in a bowl. Add the eggs and the cream and beat until smooth. Stir in the raisins and sugar. This part of the recipe can be made in advance.

When ready to eat, give the batter a good stir to loosen it. Then heat the butter and the oil in a frying pan until it sizzles and drop in tablespoonfuls of the batter. Turn the heat down slightly and fry the fritters for two minutes, or until browned on each side. They can burn easily, so do take care!

Cut the orange in half and squeeze over the fritters before serving. Eat with cream or crème fraîche.

Serves 4-6.

HOT SAUCES

HOT FUDGE SAUCE

Preparation time: 5 minutes
Cooking time: 6 minutes

4 oz/115g butter
6oz/170g soft brown sugar
7 fl oz/200ml double cream

Put all the ingredients into a pan and dissolve slowly over a gentle heat, stirring until the sugar is dissolved. Boil gently for five minutes. Cool slightly and serve over cold vanilla ice-cream or serve with fresh, juicy pears which have been peeled and cored.

Serves 4-6

HONEYED NUT SAUCE

Preparation and cooking time: 5 minutes

2oz/55g butter
2oz/55g 'soft' nuts — eg, walnuts or pinenuts
4 tbsp runny honey

Melt the butter and add the nuts to brown them slightly on a moderate heat. Reduce the heat. Next mix in the honey. Serve over creamy Greek yoghurt.

Serves 3-4.

A RUM-DO SAUCE

2 Mars bars
5 fl oz/150ml double cream
2 tbsp dark Jamaican rum

Cut up the Mars bars and melt into the cream in a small pan over a low heat. Add the rum and mix thoroughly. Serve with ripe bananas.

Serves 4.

HOT RASPBERRY SAUCE

Preparation time and cooking time: 5 minutes

14oz/400g canned raspberries
2 tsp arrowroot

Put the raspberries and their juice into a small pan and bring to the boil on the stove. Mix the arrowroot with two teaspoons of cold water and stir into the fruit. Bring to boiling point and simmer very gently for a couple of minutes. Serve over frozen ice-cream.

Serves 4.

WHISKY YOGHURT SAUCE

Preparation time: 5 minutes
Cooking time: none

7 fl oz/200ml creamy Greek yoghurt
2 tbsp runny honey
1 tbsp Scotch whisky

Mix together the cream, yoghurt and whisky and serve.
Serves 4.

Snacks on the Tracks...

...RUSH-HOUR TRAFFIC IN BIRMINGHAM WAS DISRUPTED TODAY
AFTER A MOUSE CHEWED THROUGH THE WIRING AT THE MAIN
TRAFFIC LIGHT CONTROL CENTRE. COMMUTERS FACED CHAOS
GETTING TO WORK.

(1 Sept 1992)

Are we a nation of snackers? How much food is actually home-made? You'd be surprised; a recent survey showed that while we make half of our cooked puddings ourselves, only a third of savoury dishes are home-made. Six percent of our soups are made by us and just a tiny proportion of bread — only two percent is home-made.

When it comes to snacks, this is something the commuting cook probably knows more than most about. A snatched cup of tea and slice of toast for breakfast, a sandwich for lunch and a plate of scrambled egg for supper seem to be the typical fayre for many a traveller.

Not that there's anything wrong with a snack, for it can fill a hungry gap and recharge the batteries for a few more hours. In this chapter I've put all the recipes which I don't know what to do with. Some are true snacks — such as the Brie olive bread — while others, like the Bubble and Squeak, use up leftovers and are definitely more substantial. I've also included some salads, a couple of which are very definitely meals in themselves.

All are quick and easy to make. If you're a snacker, then keep **butter, eggs, cheese** and **bread** in your kitchen and you won't go far wrong. Keep some tasty **chutney** in the cupboard, along with a selection of **pickles** and have **tomatoes** in the fridge and **fresh fruit** in the fruit bowl and you're made. Oh, and a tin of **baked beans** is never wasted, you'll need it at some stage.

CHEESY CORN EGGS

Preparation time: 5 minutes
Cooking time: 3-4 minutes

3 eggs
2oz/55g Cheddar cheese, grated
2oz/55g butter
5oz/140g small tin sweetcorn, drained
Freshly ground salt and black pepper

Beat together the eggs and cheese with a twist of salt and black pepper. Melt the butter in a saucepan and stir in the sweetcorn to heat for a minute. Add the cheesy eggs and cook for two to three minutes, stirring around to stop it sticking on the bottom of the pan. The timing really depends on how hard you like your eggs. I like my scrambled eggs slightly runny. You may want to cook yours a bit longer.
Serves 2.

EGG BREAD PLUS

Preparation time: 5 minutes
Cooking time: 5 minutes

2 eggs
1oz/30g butter
4 slices thinly cut bread
2 tbsp pesto sauce
Freshly milled salt and black pepper

Beat a couple of eggs in a flattish bowl. Season with a little salt and pepper. Spread one side of each bread slice with the pesto sauce. Put the butter on to heat in a frying pan.
Next, take the bread and dip it into the beaten egg, so it gets covered on both sides. Fry the bread until brown on one side. Then turn it over and do the same on the other side.
Serve with freshly ground black pepper.
Serves 2.

89

ANCHOVY EGGS

Preparation time: 5 minutes
Cooking time: 3-4 minutes

4 eggs
2oz/55g butter
4 anchovy fillets, drained of their oil
Freshly ground black pepper

Break the eggs into a bowl and beat with a couple of turns of black pepper. Melt the butter in a pan, add the anchovies and stir them around to break them up. Pour in the eggs and cook for a couple of minutes, stirring until they're nicely scrambled.
Serves 2.
Note: there are of course, many variations on the good old scrambled egg. For Chive Eggs, follow the above recipe but omit the anchovies and add a tablespoon of chopped chives. For Tomato Eggs, omit the anchovies and mix a teaspoon of tomato purée into the eggs. Again, cook as above.

BACON AND MUSHROOM TOPPERS

Preparation time: 5 minutes
Cooking time: 5 minutes

4 bacon rashers, snipped into small pieces
4oz/115g mushrooms, thinly sliced
2oz/55g butter
2 slices bread
2 tbsp cream cheese with chives
1 tbsp parsley, chopped
Freshly ground salt and black pepper

Melt the butter in a frying pan and fry the bacon pieces for two to three minutes. Next, add the sliced mushrooms and fry for another two minutes. Meanwhile, toast the bread and spread it with the cream cheese. Divide the bacon and mushroom mixture between the pieces of toast, piling it on top of the cheese. Finally, sprinkle the parsley on top and season.
Serves 2.

PIZZA OMELETTE

Preparation time: 10 minutes
Cooking time: 10 minutes

4 eggs, beaten
1 onion, grated
1 clove garlic, crushed
2 tbsp tapenade (olive paste)
1oz/30g butter
1 tbsp olive oil
2 medium tomatoes, sliced
3 anchovy fillets, drained of their oil
2oz/55g Cheddar cheese, grated
Freshly ground salt and black pepper

Heat the butter and oil in a frying pan and cook the onion for two minutes or until it's soft, stirring occasionally so that it doesn't burn. Meanwhile, mix the beaten eggs with the tapenade, some black pepper and a little salt. When the onion is cooked, add the anchovies and mix around for 30 seconds or so. Then add the tomatoes and heat for a further minute.

Next tip in the egg mixture and cook for two to three minutes until the bottom is set.

Sprinkle the cheese on top and put the whole thing under a hot grill for a further one to two minutes, or until the cheese starts to melt and the egg is fairly set.

Serves 2-3

Note: don't be put off by the colour. This dish is delicious.

HOT FRIED CHEESY OLIVE BREAD

Preparation time: 5 minutes
Cooking time: 6 minutes

4 slices thinly sliced bread
4oz/115g soft Brie cheese, sliced
1 tbsp tapenade (olive paste)
1 tomato, sliced
2 tbsp olive oil
Freshly ground salt and black pepper

Heat the oil in a frying pan. Spread one side of each bread slice with the olive paste. Next, make two sandwiches with the bread, the Brie and the tomato slices, putting the olive paste

side of the bread to the inside of the sandwich. Fry each sandwich in the oil for approximately two minutes on each side, or until brown and crisp.

Serves 2.

Note: if you have no olive paste, use mustard instead.

MUSHROOMS WITH ANCHOVIES

Preparation time: 5-10 minutes
Cooking time: 6 minutes

8oz/225g mushrooms, wiped and sliced
2oz/55g butter
1 tbsp olive oil
5 anchovy fillets, drained
1 clove garlic, crushed
2 tbsp red wine
4 slices bread, brown or white
Freshly ground black pepper

Heat the butter and oil and add the garlic and anchovies and cook for one minute, stirring all the time. Stir the sliced mushrooms into the pan and cook for 30 seconds or so. Add the wine, stir around and simmer gently for five minutes.

Finally, add the black pepper. A minute before the end of the cooking time, toast the bread and place a slice on each of four plates. Pile the mushroom mixture onto the toast and serve quickly before the toast goes soggy.

Serves 2-3.

BEAN-STUFFED TOMATOES

Preparation time: 5 minutes
Cooking time: 20 minutes

2 large beef tomatoes
2oz/55g Cheddar cheese, grated
5oz/140g small tin baked beans
Freshly ground salt and black pepper

Preheat oven to gas mark 6/200C/400F and warm up an ovenproof dish with a lid. Cut the top off the tomatoes and scoop out the seeds. Season the inside of the tomatoes with salt and pepper. Divide the grated cheese between the tomatoes.

Next, spoon in the beans. Place in the hot dish, put the lid on and bake for 20 minutes, taking the lid off for the last five minutes.

Season with black pepper and serve on buttered toast.

JOAN'S PIZZA

Preparation time: 10 minutes
Cooking time: 12-15 minutes

1 x 10in/25cm ready-made plain, thin pizza base
4oz/115g soft cheese and garlic spread
7oz/200g tin chopped tomatoes with herbs
4oz/115g mushrooms, sliced thinly
4oz/115g cheese, grated — Cheddar or Mozzarella
1 tbsp fresh or 1 tsp dried mixed herbs
Freshly ground salt and black pepper

Preheat oven to gas mark 7/220C/425F. Grease a baking tray. Spread soft garlic cheese over the pizza base. Drain the tomatoes of their juice and spread these over the cheese. Next arrange the sliced mushrooms on top. Sprinkle with the herbs, some salt and pepper and finish with a layer of cheese.

Bake for 12-15 minutes or until the pastry looks crisp and the cheese is browned and bubbling.

Serves 2.

Joan is a friend who works in the make-up department at ITN. As well as giving me recipes, she was always there on newsreading days to rebuild me when I staggered off the train, hot, tired and hassled. And talking of things tired, left-over vegetables can be a great help to the commuting cook. They can be mixed with stock and liquidised to make a hearty soup, or, if you've lots of mashed potato, they can form the basis of the next two recipes.

BUBBLE AND SQUEAK

Preparation time: 5 minutes
Cooking time: 10-15 minutes

1lb/450g cooked potato and any leftover vegetables you have left, such as carrots, cabbage etc.
3oz/85g butter
Freshly ground salt and black pepper

Mix the potatoes and the vegetables, cutting up those that are too big. Season with salt and pepper. Melt the butter in a frying pan and fry the vegetable mix, pressing it down so that it covers the whole pan. Cook for six to seven minutes and then turn the whole lot over to brown the other side. When it's heated through and crusty on the outside, eat with some good pickle.

Serves 2-3.

Note: this is delicious and with a fried egg on the top, deliciously fattening too.

SPICY CORNED BEEF MIX

Preparation time: 15 minutes
Cooking time: 10 minutes

1 small onion, grated
8oz/225g cooked potatoes — either mashed, or boiled and roughly chopped
7oz/200g tin chopped tomatoes with herbs
8oz/225g tin corned beef, roughly chopped
1 tbsp olive oil
1 tbsp Worcestershire sauce
Freshly ground salt and black pepper

Heat the oil and fry the onion for two minutes until soft, stirring so that it doesn't burn. Next add the tomatoes, potato, corned beef and Worcestershire sauce and mix well. Cook for five minutes. Check for seasoning and serve.

Serves 2-3

NUTTY COURGETTES

Preparation time: 10 minutes
Cooking time: 15 minutes

1lb/450g courgettes, wiped and chopped into ¼-inch slices
1oz/30g butter with garlic and herbs
1 tbsp fresh herbs, chopped, such as parsley or chives
2oz/55g walnuts, chopped
2oz/55g Cheddar cheese, grated
1oz/30g fresh Parmesan cheese, grated
5 fl oz/150ml fromage frais
1 tbsp lemon juice
Freshly ground salt and black pepper

Preheat oven to gas mark 5/200C/380F. Heat the butter in a frying pan and fry courgettes for three to four minutes. Next, add some salt and pepper, the Cheddar cheese, herbs, nuts, lemon juice and mix gently around.

Place it all in an ovenproof dish. Spoon over the fromage frais and sprinkle the Parmesan cheese on top. Bake, uncovered, in the oven for 10-12 minutes or until browned.

Serves 3.

POTTED CHICKEN

Preparation time: 10 minutes
Cooking time: none

8oz/225g cooked chicken, roughly chopped
1¹/₂ tbsp lemon juice
4 oz/115g cottage cheese with chives
1 tbsp chives, or spring onion tops
1 tbsp parsley
5 fl oz/150g creamy plain Greek yoghurt
Freshly ground salt and black pepper

Put the chicken in the food processor with the cottage cheese, parsley and chives and whizz until you have a smooth mixture. Add the yoghurt and lemon juice and whizz again. Check for seasoning and serve with a few chives over the top. Eat with crusty bread and some pickles.

Serves 2.

AVOCADO AND BACON SALAD

Preparation time: 5-10 minutes
Cooking time: 5 minutes

1 ripe avocado, peeled, stoned and cubed
4 slices smoked bacon, snipped into ¹/₂-inch pieces
1 tbsp red pesto sauce
1 tbsp olive oil
Salt and freshly ground pepper

Heat the oil and fry the bacon bits for two to three minutes until crisp. Meanwhile, arrange the avocado cubes on two plates and place half a tablespoon of red pesto sauce at the side of each. When the bacon is cooked, divide it between the plates, arranging it over the avocado. Grind on some black pepper and serve.

Serves 2.

HOT CHICKEN LIVER SALAD

Preparation time: 10 minutes
Cooking time: 5 minutes

8oz/225g chicken livers, drained, trimmed and cut into bite-sized pieces
1 garlic clove, crushed
1oz/30g butter
2 tbsp olive oil
1 small handful thyme leaves, or 1 tsp dried
1 x 7oz/200g bag mixed salad leaves
3 tbsp French dressing
Freshly ground salt and black pepper

Heat the oil and butter in a small frying pan and add the garlic and thyme and stir around for a minute, being careful not to burn the garlic. Next, add the chicken liver pieces and cook quickly for two to three minutes, tossing them around so they brown evenly. Meanwhile empty the bag of salad leaves into a shallow bowl and toss them in the French dressing.

Remove the livers from the pan and place them on top of the leaves, with all the pan juices too. Season with salt and pepper and serve.

Serves 2.

Note: if you don't like your livers pink inside, cook them for a couple of minutes more. If in doubt, take one out and test it! Also, if your livers are frozen - and they usually are - don't forget to take them out of the freezer the night before and leave them to defrost in the fridge.

GRILLED BUTTERY TOMATOES

Preparation time: 5 minutes
Cooking time: 5 minutes

4 large beefsteak tomatoes, halved
3oz/85g packet herb and garlic butter, cut into eight pieces
2 tbsp fresh herbs, chopped
Freshly ground salt and black pepper

Turn on the grill to high. Arrange the tomato halves on an heatproof tray. Make a slit through the middle of each tomato, almost going down to the bottom, but not actually piercing the skin and push a piece of butter into each slit. Grind on some salt and pepper and grill for four to five minutes, or until soft and hot.

Sprinkle with the fresh herbs and don't forget to serve with some bread to mop up the buttery juices.

Serves 4.

PRAWNS AU GRATIN

Preparation time: 10 minutes
Cooking time: 15 minutes

8oz/225g shelled prawns
5 fl oz/150ml double cream
1 tbsp parsley, chopped
1 egg, hard-boiled and mashed
4oz/115g Gruyère cheese, grated
1oz/30g butter
1 tsp French mustard
Freshly ground salt and black pepper

Preheat oven to gas mark 5/190C/375F. Grease four ramekin dishes with a quarter of the butter. Heat the remaining butter, cream, mustard and parsley in a saucepan. Add the cheese, chopped egg, prawns and some black pepper. Remove from the heat and divide between the ramekins.

Cook in the oven for 10-12 minutes or until brown and bubbling. Serve with brown bread and butter.

Serves 4 as a small snack, 2 as a hearty one!

SMART SALAD

Preparation time: 10-15 minutes
Cooking time: none

1 small melon, seeded and chopped into bite-sized pieces
7oz/200g seedless small grapes
Half a cucumber, peeled, seeded and chopped
6 tbsp French dressing
4 tbsp single cream
1 tbsp mint, chopped
Freshly ground black pepper

Mix the fruit in a bowl. Mix the French dressing with the mint and cream and stir carefully into the fruit. Season well with some black pepper.

Serves 4.

CHEESE AND APPLE PESTO SALAD

Preparation time: 10 minutes
Cooking time: none

1 x midget gem lettuce, divided and washed
5 fl oz/150ml creamy Greek yoghurt
3 tbsp mayonnaise
1 tbsp pesto sauce
2 eating apples, cored and diced, but not peeled
8oz/225g Edam cheese, cubed
4 spring onion tops, snipped
Freshly ground salt and black pepper

Mix the mayonnaise and the yoghurt with the pesto. Season with pepper, and salt, if needed. Mix the apple cubes and the cheese cubes into the yoghurt dressing. Place on a bed of lettuce leaves and snip the onion tops over this. Season with black pepper and serve.

Serves 2.

STILTON AND TOMATO SALAD

Preparation time: 5 minutes
Cooking time: none

4oz/115g Stilton cheese, crumbled
8oz/225g tomatoes, sliced
6 spring onion tops, snipped
4 tbsp French dressing
Freshly ground salt and black pepper

Arrange the tomatoes on a plate, not overlapping if possible. Crumble on the cheese and spoon over the dressing. Sprinkle on the spring onion tops.

Grind on black pepper and serve.

Serves 2.

WALNUT SALAD

Preparation time: 5 minutes
Cooking time: none

2 x midget gem lettuces, divided and washed
2oz/55g walnut pieces, chopped
1 Granny Smith's apple, cored and thinly sliced, but not
**   peeled**
5oz/150ml carton soured cream
Freshly ground salt and black pepper

Mix everything carefully around, season and serve.
Serves 2.

SALMON AND CHICK PEA SALAD

Preparation time: 5-10 minutes
Cooking time: none

7oz/200g tinned salmon, drained and flaked
14oz/400g canned chick peas, rinsed and drained
1 red-skinned salad onion, finely sliced
4 small, sweet tomatoes, quartered
1 tbsp fresh herbs, chopped
1 tbsp lemon juice
3 tbsp olive oil
Freshly ground salt and black pepper

Mix the salmon and the chick peas in a bowl. Next add the
onion, tomatoes, olive oil, herbs and lemon juice. Mix it all
gently around and season to taste. Eat with crusty bread and
butter.
Serves 4.

Express Service...

TEN COMMUTERS WHO BET £100 THAT BR COULD RUN 11 OUT
OF 20 TRAINS ON THE 18:10 SERVICE FROM LIVERPOOL
STREET TO NORWICH ON TIME, LOSE THEIR BET ...

The Times, December 1991

I've talked already about the sort of equipment which might be useful to a commuting cook, such as the food processor, but there is another piece of equipment that I've found really useful when I'm hard pressed for time — a **microwave** oven. Mine is an old friend and is getting on a bit, but it has a permanent place in my kitchen and I really don't think I could cope without it. Most modern pure microwave ovens, like mine, (that is, not combination or convection) are rated at 650-700 watts output and should yours have a different rating, ensure that you check the manufacturer's directions regarding cooking times. If your oven is less than the 650-700 watt output, then the following guidelines may help to determine cooking times:

1. For every minute of cooking time add 45 seconds for ovens with a 400-watt rating.
2. For every minute of cooking time add 25 seconds for ovens with a 500-watt rating.
3. For every minute of cooking time add 10 seconds for ovens with a 600-watt rating.

If nothing else, your microwave will come in very handy to **defrost** whatever you've forgotten to take out of the freezer before you left for work. It's also great for **reheating** food quickly and, of course, for **baking potatoes**. A microwave can do much, much more. For example, it can...

Melt butter: 1oz/30g takes approx 20 seconds on high.

Soften butter or margarine for spreading, or if you want to make a cake: allow approx 8 seconds on high for 4oz/115g butter.

Soften cream cheese for spreading: give it 20-30 seconds on defrost.

Melt chocolate: 2oz/55g of broken-up chocolate on medium for approximately two minutes.

Dissolve gelatine: place the gelatine in two tablespoons of water and leave for a couple of minutes to 'sponge', then cook on high for approximately 30 seconds.

Soften ice-cream: only try this with ice-cream straight from the freezer, not the soft-scoop type which is quite soft enough. Give a one-litre tub 30 seconds or so on medium, but check constantly. Do 5 seconds at a time and test with your finger!

Defrost frozen pastry: a small packet will take two minutes on the lowest defrost setting; a large packet will take four minutes. Defrost it in its wrapper to prevent hot spots.

Defrost bread: give a slice 10 seconds on low.

Freshen bread that's seen better days: sprinkle some drops of water over an old loaf and give it 15-20 seconds on high.

Toast nuts: such as almonds; shell and place on a microwaveproof plate and give them between two to five minutes on high. Check every minute to make sure nothing is burning.

Dry breadcrumbs: a slice of bread will take two to three minutes on high to dry. Then you can crumble or grate it into breadcrumbs. Keep an eye on it as it dries to prevent hot spots.

Make citrus fruits juicier: prick the skins of oranges and lemons and put them on high for 20-30 seconds to get more juice when you squeeze them.

Rescue crystallised honey: remove the lid of the jar and allow 30 seconds to 1 minute on high or until clear again.

Heat baby food in jars: remove the tops if metallic, allow 30 seconds on high and then test. Thereafter, allow increments of 5 seconds to get the correct temperature. Since food continues to cook after coming out of a micro, allow the baby food to stand for a while, then stir well and test the temperature again before you give it to your baby!

Dry herbs: put the leaves between two sheets of kitchen paper and microwave on high for three to four minutes or until dry and crumbly.

Bring dried mushrooms back to life: place the dried mushrooms in a bowl of boiling water and cook in the microwave for two to three minutes on high.

Heat up plates: but only so long they are microwave-proof, have no gilt on them and are not cracked. Allow one minute on high.

I am now going to give you a few examples of dishes that can be made in the microwave. Follow the manufacturer's instructions for precise cooking times, which will vary dependent on the quantities being cooked

VEGETABLES

Whether fresh or frozen, cooking these is one of the strengths of a microwave. Because you don't need much water, the vegetables keep their goodness and colour and are less likely to go soggy.

FROZEN PEAS

Add a little butter. Cover and cook as directed. Stir during cooking.

FROZEN SPINACH

Place in a dish, but do not add extra water. Cover and cook as directed, or until defrosted and hot. Stir halfway through.

CARROTS FOR A SALAD

Cut the carrots into sticks and place in a dish with a little water. Cover with cling film, making steam holes in the top and microwave as directed, or until tender but still with some bite. Allow to cool and serve in a salad.

BROCOLLI FLORETS

For a side vegetable, or a salad: place in a dish with the heads of the florets pointing in to the middle. Add a little water, cover and cook as directed.

AUBERGINES

Cut off the stalk end and pierce several times with a fork. Wrap in kitchen paper and bake whole on high for between four and six minutes, turning once during the cooking.

When cooked, cool slightly, mash and add lemon juice, herbs and seasoning for a delicious dip.

CORN ON THE COB

Trim and cook, covered, for four to five minutes on high in two tablespoons of water. Leave to stand before serving with melted butter.

BAKED POTATOES

Scrub the potatoes, prick the skins several times and lay them on kitchen paper. Allow six to eight minutes on high for two 6oz/180g potatoes. When they're cooked, fill them with all sorts of delicious things, such as tuna and sweetcorn, or cheese and pickle. The microwave does tend to make the skins soft so if you like your baked potatoes with a crisper skin, and you have the time, you can always finish them off with 10 minutes at a high heat in a conventional oven.

Note: if you cook vegetables this way, don't use salt during the microwaving, since it can make things a bit tough. You can, of course, always add it later. Also, if you're cooking vegetables with skins, always pierce the skin with a knife or fork to stop any bursting in the oven.

FRUIT

Like vegetables, fruit cooks well since it keeps its shape and colour and doesn't mush, as long as you don't overdo it. If you want a soft purée, then obviously, cook it for a bit longer.

BAKED APPLES

Core and fill an eating apple with dried fruit, sugar and butter. Score round the centre of the fruit, to stop it bursting. Cover and cook for three minutes on high.

Baked Pear

Peel, core and cut in half. Put in a dish with the thin ends pointing into the middle. Pour over a couple of tablespoons of fruit juice, either orange or apple, and sprinkle on some ground cinnamon. Cook for 3 minutes on high.

Porridge

No more standing and stirring at a hot stove! Use a high-sided dish to make sure it doesn't boil over in the microwave. Two rounded tablespoons of oats with fl oz/150ml of water, a pinch of salt, a good mix around and 90 seconds on high should do the trick.

Fish

Fish is wonderful done in the microwave, since it tends to keep its texture and stays lovely and moist. Don't overdo the time, though! Remember, fish will carry on cooking slightly when you take it out of the oven. Always cover fish when you're cooking it in the microwave. I use clingfilm and make small holes in the top to let the steam escape. As for cooking times, well, they vary depending on the size and thickness of the fish, but generally speaking, a salmon cutlet could take three to four minutes on high, whereas something thinner like a plaice fillet may only need two minutes or so.

Welsh Rarebit

Preparation time: 5 minutes
Cooking and standing time: 3 minutes

2oz/55g butter
1 tsp English mustard
4oz/115g Cheddar cheese, grated
1 tsp Worcestershire sauce
4 slices bread
Freshly ground salt and black pepper

Melt the butter as I've suggested. Add the mustard, cheese and Worcestershire sauce and mix. Microwave on high for 30 seconds. Make the toast and divide the cheesy mixture between the toasts. Put back in the microwave for a further 30 seconds or until bubbling. Season and serve.

Serves 4 as a starter, 2 as a snack.

CHICKEN AND COURGETTES

Preparation time: 10 minutes
Cooking and standing time: 8 minutes

11b/450g chicken, cut into strips
11b/450g courgettes, wiped and cut into ¼-inch slices
8oz/225g mushrooms, wiped and cut into ¼-inch slices
4 tbsp dry sherry
2 tbsp soy sauce
5 fl oz/150 ml fromage frais
Freshly ground salt and black pepper

Put everything except the fromage frais into a large, microwaveproof dish and add some pepper. Cover with cling film and make slits in the film to allow the steam to escape. Microwave on high for four minutes, giving it all a good stir halfway through the cooking time.

Leave to stand for a few minutes and then mix in the fromage frais. Check the seasoning, since it may need some salt. There may be a lot of juice, so lift the chicken out with a slotted spoon and add sauce to suit.

Serve with a salad and new potatoes.

Serves 4.

PASTA SAUCE (SPINACH AND ANCHOVY)

Preparation time: 5 minutes
Cooking time: 12 minutes

2oz/55g butter
8oz/225g frozen chopped spinach (no need to defrost)
7oz/200g cream cheese
2 tbsp single cream or milk
1oz/30g fresh Parmesan cheese, grated
5 anchovy fillets, drained of oil
Freshly ground salt and black pepper

Put the butter into a large, microwaveproof dish and give it 30 seconds on high or until it melts. Add the spinach and cover the dish with clingfilm, making slits in the top. Microwave on high for five minutes, stirring around halfway through the cooking time.

Add the cream cheese, the milk or cream, the Parmesan cheese and the anchovies and cook for a further five minutes on low. Adjust seasoning and mix into cooked pasta.

Serves 4.

KIPPER WITH TOMATO

Preparation time: 5 minutes
Cooking time: 3 minutes

2 kipper fillets, each about 6oz/170g
1 tsp lemon juice
Freshly ground black pepper
2 tomatoes

Place the kippers on a plate and sprinkle with lemon juice and black pepper. Halve the tomatoes and place next to the kippers.

Cover with kitchen paper and cook on high for two to three minutes or until steaming hot.

Serve on hot buttered toast.

Serves 2.

HERBED PLAICE

Preparation time: 5-10 minutes
Cooking time: 6 minutes

1lb/450g plaice fillets, skin off
1oz/30g butter
7oz/200g tin chopped tomatoes and herbs
6 spring onion tops, snipped finely
2 tbsp fresh herbs, chopped, such as parsley and dill
1 tbsp lemon juice
Freshly ground salt and black pepper

Butter a large microwaveproof plate and arrange the tinned tomatoes and the chopped spring onion tops on the bottom. Next place the fish on top of this, trying to get them all in a single layer. Put the herbs evenly on top of this and sprinkle on the lemon juice. Season with the pepper and cook for three to four minutes on high.

Add salt at the end to taste.
Serves 3.

SPICED CHICK PEAS

Preparation time: 10 minutes
Cooking time: 5-10 minutes

2 x 14oz/400g tinned or canned chick peas
16oz/450g tinned chopped tomatoes
1 onion, grated
2 garlic cloves, crushed
1 tsp paprika
1 tsp turmeric
1 tsp ground cumin
½ tsp chilli powder
2 tbsp olive oil
Chopped coriander to garnish
Freshly ground salt and black pepper

Put the oil in a large microwaveproof dish and add the onion, garlic, paprika, turmeric, cumin and chilli powder. Cover with cling film, making slits in the top and cook on high for two to three minutes, stirring halfway through. Next add the tomatoes and chick peas and mix well. Cook on high for three minutes, again, stirring halfway through.

Allow to stand for a minute or so and season to taste with salt and pepper. Serve with the chopped coriander snipped over. Eat with a salad.
Serves 4.
Note: this is delicious cold too.

BAKED APPLES

Preparation time: 5 minutes
Cooking and standing time: 10 minutes

2oz/55g raisins
2oz/55g brown sugar
4 medium cooking apples
1oz/30g butter
4 tbsp water

Mix up the raisins and brown sugar. Core the apples and

make a thin cut right round the middle of them to stop them splitting when cooking. Put them into a microwaveproof dish and fill with the raisins and brown sugar. Dot the butter over the top of the apples and pour the water round the sides. Microwave on high for six to eight minutes, or until they are cooked.

Allow to stand for four minutes before serving. Eat with custard, which you can make whilst the apples are standing.

Serves 4.

MICROWAVE CUSTARD

Preparation time: 5 minutes
Cooking time: 4 minutes

2 rounded tbsp custard powder
2 tbsp caster sugar
1pt/570ml milk

In a microwaveproof jug, mix the custard powder and sugar with three tablespoons of the milk until smooth. Then add the rest of the milk and mix again, making sure there are no lumps!

Microwave on high for four minutes, or until thick, stirring every minute.

Serves 4.

KIWI SPONGES

Preparation time: 10-15 minutes
Cooking time: 5 minutes

2oz/55g soft serve margarine
2oz/55g brown sugar
2oz/55g self-raising flour
2 drops vanilla essence
2 eggs, beaten
4 Kiwi fruits, peeled and sliced
2 tbsp clear honey
1oz/30g walnuts, chopped
1 tbsp lemon juice

Grease four ramekin dishes and line the bases with greaseproof paper. Mix the margarine and sugar. When well-blended, add the flour, essence and eggs and mix well until smooth. Take two Kiwi fruit slices and arrange them at the bottom of the 4 ramekin dishes.

Divide the cake mixture between the four dishes, smoothing it out on top of the Kiwi fruits. Cover with kitchen paper and cook on medium for three minutes.

When the mixture firms up and begins to leave the sides of the dishes slightly, bring them out of the micro and leave them to stand for a few minutes.

Meanwhile, put the honey, walnuts and lemon juice into a cup and cook on high for 20 seconds. Turn the puddings out onto four plates and remove the greaseproof paper. Spoon the honey sauce over the pudding and serve with the extra Kiwi fruits.

Serves 4.

POACHED APRICOT SALAD

6oz/170g dried apricots
8 fl oz/250 ml fresh orange juice
2 tbsp apricot brandy

Put the apricots in a microwaveproof bowl and add the orange juice. Cover with clingfilm, make slits in the top and microwave on high for 10 minutes. Leave to stand a few minutes and then add the brandy. Eat with crème fraîche.

Serves 4.

TOASTIES AND FILLINGS

The other kitchen gadget you might find useful is a **toasted sandwich maker**, especially if you are a snacky type of person. It's probably worth buying one just to try out the wonderful range of fillings you can make. They all taste delicious and only take a few minutes to make.

Follow the manufacturers instructions for filling quantities and cooking instructions and enjoy fillings like:

SMOKED SALMON AND CUCUMBER WITH TOMATO AND MINT YOGHURT

Wafer thin slices of salmon and thinly sliced cucumber with a tsp of tomato and mint yoghurt in the centre.

To make tomato and mint yoghurt: 1 small carton of natural yoghurt mixed with 2 dessert spoons of tomato ketchup, 2 tsps mint sauce, a pinch of caster sugar and a tsp of lemon juice.

TUNA AND MAYONNAISE

Simply drain tinned tuna and mix with mayonnaise to dropping consistency.

ROAST TURKEY AND CRANBERRY SAUCE

Wafer thin slices of roast turkey with a tsp of apricot chutney on top.

BAKED BEANS AND CHEESE

Speaks for itself. Some canned baked beans and grated cheese of your choice!

BLUE CHEESE AND PEAR

Crumbled blue cheese, such as Stilton, Danish Blue or Dolcelatta and thin slices of peeled and cored fresh pear.

CHICKEN AND SWEETCORN IN MAYONNAISE

Chopped cooked chicken mixed with tinned, drained, sweetcorn and mayonnaise to a dropping consistency.

ROAST BEEF AND PEPPERS WITH TOMATO CHUTNEY

Wafer thin slices of roast beef, thinly sliced and diced red or green peppers with a tsp of tomato chutney on top.

HAM AND DIJON MUSTARD

Wafer thin slices of ham with a tsp of Dijon mustard on top.

PRAWNS AND LIME MAYONNAISE

Cooked, peeled, prawns mixed with mayonnaise and a squeeze of lime juice to taste, again to a dropping consistency.
Notes:

1. Dropping consistency: Mixed to a consistency that does not easily fall off the spoon.
2. If possible, use Baxter's chutney. It is quite simply avenues ahead of any alternatives.

Don't Panic!

POLICE WERE CALLED TO DISPERSE ANGRY COMMUTERS AT FENCHURCH STREET STATION, LONDON, AFTER TRAINS ARE CANCELLED DUE TO SNOW.

The Times, February 1991

This is an easy chapter for me to write, as I can look back at my many culinary disasters over the years! You learn by your mistakes, they say, or do you? All I'm trying to say is don't pull the communication cord!

When we were living in Africa, much of the cooking was done outside on a large stove. The wood used for burning came from the local rubber trees and I remember how it used to smoke like crazy and flavour everything it touched. It meant, of course, that not only did we have smoked guinea fowl, we also had smoked okra, smoked yam and often, smoked spinach, which has a most unusual flavour, I can tell you.

I still have my share of smoky food but I really don't know the answer to the problem of burning the food, unless you're prepared to sit and watch it from start to finish, which of course, the commuting cook has no time to do. One solution is to get a timer and rely on that.

Other major disasters I've coped with include putting sugar instead of salt into a savoury dish and getting the timings completely wrong. In these cases, too, there's not a lot you can do about it and remember that real disasters involve things like losing the only corkscrew! And, although annoying, unlike pulling a real communication cord, you're not likely to get fined for making a mistake in the kitchen, are you? So let's see what we can do when things go wrong.

The chocolate you're melting has gone hard and grainy

You have overheated it or let some boiling water near it! Chocolate is very temperamental as most star turns are. If you see it turning grainy, take it off the stove and beat in a nut of butter. With a bit of luck, it should smooth out again. Do chop chocolate evenly since that helps to melt it quickly and the less time it spends on the heat, the better. Do not let water near it...ever!

Your pasta sticks to the pan and to itself

No problem! Always make sure that you add a tablespoon of vegetable oil to the boiling water before you add the pasta.

Too much salt in the soup

Haven't we all at one stage or other? Peel a couple of potatoes and cook them in the soup for ten minutes or so. With a bit of luck, they will take some of the salt out of the soup.

You've burned the soup

Take it off the stove and pour off what you can into a fresh pan, without taking any of the burnt bits from the bottom. With luck, it shouldn't pick up the burnt flavour.

You've burned the cake a little on top

Sieve icing sugar over the top to make it look nicer.

You've burned the cake badly

Cut off the burnt bits and use what's left in the middle for a trifle.

To keep a fresh lettuce or refresh a limp lettuce

Separate the leaves, wash and dry them. Put them in a

plastic bag, tie it up and put it in the bottom of the fridge. The lettuce should crisp up nicely.

TO MAKE DOUBLE CREAM GO FURTHER

Add a tablespoon of milk to every quarter-pint you whip.

NO CRÈME FRAÎCHE

One tablespoon of natural yoghurt added to a quarter-pint of double cream makes a reasonable substitute.

NO SOUR CREAM

Mix a quarter-pint of cream with a teaspoon of lemon juice.

YOU'VE TOO MUCH CREAM

If it's double, add a tablespoon of milk to each quarter-pint, whip it and freeze in a plastic box. It'll keep for a month or so and is ready whipped for your next pudding. If it's single cream, use it up in coffee or add to soups or sauces.

WATERY SCRAMBLED EGG

You've most likely cooked it too quickly. Strain off the liquid and add a knob of butter.

NO SELF-RAISING FLOUR

Easy. Just use plain flour and baking powder. To 8oz/225g plain flour, add 2 level teaspoons of baking powder.

TEARS FROM PEELING ONIONS

Peel them under water and you'll stay dry-eyed.

ONION OR GARLIC BREATH

Chew some fresh parsley to smell sweet again.

ONION SMELLS ON YOUR HANDS

Again, use parsley and rub it between your hands.

YOU'VE BEEN SEPARATING EGGS AND HAVE GOT YOLK IN YOUR WHITES

If it's just a tiny bit, don't panic. It should still whip up. If it's a lot, you may have to abandon the job and use the eggs you've already cracked for something like an omelette. To avoid this problem though, it may be worth using separate dishes for each egg you crack, so if anything spoils, it's only the one egg and not half a dozen. It may mean washing 6 small dishes afterwards, but that's probably preferable to having to make omelettes for the rest of the week!

NO SUGAR

Use honey, but only half the amount, as honey is much sweeter.

HARD BOILED EGG (FOR SALADS)

To save time, how often have you boiled eggs the night before for the salad the following day? Then you find to your embarrassment that when the eggs are sliced, they look aged with unsightly black, blue and grey rings staring straight back at you. If you follow these tips, I can guarantee perfect hard-boiled eggs every time.

(i) Place eggs into boiling water. This should be gently boiling, just slightly more than a simmer.

(ii) Bring back to a gentle boil and cook for 8-10 minutes.

(iii) Refresh until cold (in their shells) under running cold water.

NB. If a high temperature or prolonged cooking time are used to boil eggs, iron within the yolk and sulphur compounds within the white are released to form the unsightly blackish grey-blue ring around the yolk. Stale eggs will also produce this effect no matter what you do.

115

A GUIDE TO EGG SIZES

Pre-EC Sizes	EC Sizes	Weight
Large	Size 1	70 g or over
	Size 2	65—70g
Standard	Size 3	60—65g
	Size 4	55—60g
Medium	Size 5	50—55g
	Size 6	45—50g
Small	Size 7	Under 45g

IF AN EGG CRACKS WHILE BEING BOILED

Remove it immediately, wrap in tin foil and return to the pan, or add a few drops of vinegar to the water.

WINE

Wine nearly always improves a soup. However, it will tend to highlight any saltiness, so if this is already a problem, do not add wine.

Wine always needs to be cooked — raw wine in a cooked dish is not a good idea. It can curdle soups with a heavy milk content. If this happens, continue to cook and generally it will correct itself. If not, add a little double cream, which will normally bring it together. If all else fails whack it in the blender and beat the living daylights out of it.

REMOVING FAT

Sorry to disappoint those slimmers reading but I can only advise on sauces. If a sauce is greasy or has that frustrating layer of butter or fat floating on the top, soak it up with sheets of paper kitchen towel laid over the sauce, (if using gas take it off the heat first, or you may remove your kitchen as well as the fat). The paper will absorb the fat and leave the sauce behind. Alternatively, the best way, if you have the time, is to chill the sauce. This will congeal the fat, which can then be scraped off with a spoon.

PASTRY PATCHING

This sounds like a bygone country craft, but it happens in the most modern kitchens. You make the perfect pastry and then it tears as you roll it out. Follow the next few points to reduce the damage.

(i) It helps to lift it over a rolling pin rather than with your hands.

(ii) If you are lining a flan case use little bits of pastry to patch the cracks or tears. Moistening the base with milk or beaten egg before applying the patch and pressing it down.

(iii) Use the pastry trimmings to disguise a multitude of sins on a pie top by careful decoration. A leaf is the simplest and often the most effective option, however, little pastry balls are even easier. Be adventurous with your trimmings, they can cover all the cracks and look very impressive.

TO PREVENT SPOONS STICKING

Dip a spoon in milk before spooning batter, milk pudding or cake mixture. This prevents sticking.

WHEN MAKING SAUCES

Use a wooden spoon because a metal one may discolour the sauce, particularly white based ones.

Why do we do it ...?

THE LONGEST TRAFFIC JAM EVERY REPORTED STRETCHED 109
MILES FROM LYONS TO PARIS IN 1980. THE LONGEST BRITISH
TRAFFIC JAMS WERE TWO OF 40 MILES — ON THE M1 IN
1985, AND ON THE M6 IN LANCASHIRE IN 1987.

Guinness Book of Records

Commute, that is. Why indeed? We all need to work but there are times when it just doesn't seem worth the effort. We do tend to put up with so many hardships on the way to and from work so that an incident-free trip seems almost memorable. These are reflections on a year's commuting between London and the Borders which I recorded in my diaries during 1988-89.

Monday, August 8, 1988.
07.44 Carlisle to London.
The train rolls into Carlisle dead on time. The platform is chock-a-block with holidaymakers. Sit down in carriage and realise I've made a big mistake by sitting right over the wheels. Don't particularly want a bumpy ride ... then hear a few rows away three very loud Scotsmen talking excitedly about a rugby game they've been to. It's too early in the morning for all that, so I move down the carriage. I sit in peace until I realise I'm by the automatic door which keeps (automatically) opening by itself.

It creates a huge draught, so I get up and try to shut it. No luck, it stays open. Well, I won't move again, it's too full, even though the intercom is buzzing uncontrollably above my head. Try to go to buffet but cannot get along the corridor for folk standing. We are only at Lancaster and the train is already heaving. At Warrington, the guard apologises for the severe congestion. I really feel sorry for him as well as the people standing — he's getting dog's abuse from them. At Crewe, however, they tell all the old folk and those with young

118

children to go and sit in first class. Go for a cup of tea but, again, can't get near the buffet. Nice BR man in restaurant gets me a drink from the side door. He apologises for the lack of a trolley, but the boiler has broken down ...

Mon, August 22, 1988.
07.44 Carlisle to London.
Again, get train to London. Again it is very crowded. The guard tells me this is a common problem on this particular train and that they keep asking for a relief train, 'But you know what it's like ...' I certainly do, but at least I have a seat, unlike the poor folk who have to stand from Preston. Still, we arrive in London on time and if you have a seat, life is good. I have another bugbear, though — personal stereos! What a con because they're not personal at all! All the way down I sat and listened to the drumming and the squeaking of some awful music from a man sitting several seats down the carriage! Next drama is when dog on the train bites another man's leg ... great debate ensues ... should dog be on the train at all? Go to the buffet, unwisely as it turned out, because when I come back, there are two of the people who had been standing, fighting over my seat. Someone else has taken my newspapers. Retrieve my seat politely but firmly. Give the seat next to me away — I am sure she's gone. It all settles down, then the lady I thought had gone returns and is very displeased to see her seat taken. Displace new owner, reinstate old ... Compare notes on tapestry cushion I as making with man opposite. He also does tapestry ... and works on the oil rigs ...

Thursday, September 29, 1988.
19.30 London to Carlisle.
It looks very busy tonight so I go first class. Look forward to a meal on the train. But the steward is very embarrassed because they only have 20 meals on board and there are about 50 wanting to eat! The man in front rants and raves. He only bought a first-class ticket to be sure of getting a meal. We end up with sandwiches and an address to complain to about the catering. I talk to a fellow passenger, a man who sells stamps and is going up to buy a collection from Preston. We're lucky he says, the previous week he was on a train with no power, so not only was there no food, there was no heat and no light! The irate man is still shouting: 'If I ran my business like this, I'd be bankrupt in 10 days!' I get a sandwich — bacon, lettuce and tomato and it's delicious. I go back for a prawn one, which is soggy. Serves me right for being greedy ... however we arrive on time!

Wednesday, October 12, 1988.
13.48 Carlisle to London.

New timetable is in force. We've lost a couple of weekday trains, but the service is generally the same, thank God. I don't know how I'd get to work otherwise. Am not looking forward to going back to London after 12 days off and my heart sinks at the station. However, they seem to be doing improvements to the fabric of the station — does this mean that Carlisle is not to be run down after all?! Hurray! Train comes in from Glasgow and I sit over the wheels, but it's busy so I stay put. There's a camera crew opposite, so I keep my head down. Meanwhile we are treated to a song from a drunken man who walks up and down the carriage singing cockney songs ... it's quite entertaining. My only complaint is that I sit under the tannoy and each time the guard makes an announcement, he blasts my head off ... 'Ladies and gentlemen, we are now arriving at Rockerby ...' Rockerby? Oh, Rugby ... the drunken man's mood has now turned and he starts getting aggressive with passengers. He's last seen threatening some lad who will probably end up thumping him.

Monday, October 31, 1988.
07.20 London to Carlisle.

Superb train, quiet, clean, quick and warm. Trolley service at seat too. Best trip I've had for yonks. On time, too, at Carlisle. Thank you BR — I take it all back!

Monday, January 2, 1989.
15.51 Carlisle to London.

Paid the supplement and sat in first class. Very crowded. Suddenly the lights go out and the guard comes on the intercom to ask if anyone has a torch! If they do, could they please bring it to the buffet. Later, I peer down the corridor and see that the torch has been duly found and the catering crew, bless them, are still soldiering on, selling sandwiches in the dark. One man points out that with all the stops between here and London, they should be able to pick up a lantern on the way.

It seems early for the dark, but it's the winter months. Guard tries to move a woman who couldn't find a seat in second class and has come to first class and is refusing to pay the supplement. He tells her, BR do not guarantee you a seat. 'What do you expect me to do', she says, 'sit in the dark, on the floor?' Others around her mutter their support and the guard leaves well alone. We arrive at Euston 20 minutes late because of operational problems.

Friday, 27 January, 1989.
19.30 London to Carlisle.
Got on in fear because I hadn't booked and it was busy. But I did find a seat ... but why are there three first-class carriages which all look empty? Realise have made mistake by sitting in rickety carriage, the bumpiest, most rattling thing I've ever been in. Old rolling stock, I think — very old! Also carriage gets unbearably hot as heating is stuck. Asked guard about it and he sympathised, but said it was old 'rolling stock'. While we sweltered, the man on the right sniffed loudly all the way whilst opposite I have two yuppies going to Oxenholme for the weekend who talk loudly about the stock market and bottles of bubbly consumed at a lunch party.

By now the train is full and bursting with folk in the corridors. I wouldn't go all that way without a seat. I'd go into one of the empty first-class carriages and not budge! It's funny, travelling first class as I have been doing recently, I don't think I see the problems. This is like a cattle truck! Oh, another large sniff from the man and the yuppies are now discussing share prices. It was our third lead on the news at 5.40 tonight, so I don't want to hear any more about it ... I eventually go and stand in the corridor, driven out by the sniffer and the heat ...

Wednesday, February 1, 1989.
07.44 Carlisle to London.
Nice comfortable train ... fast, slept all the way.

Friday, February 17, 1989.
18.30 London to Carlisle.
Went first class and sit very near buffet so if they only bring a few meals on, I'll have a chance of getting one! Meet an agony aunt and a psychoanalyst and a former friend from the BBC. We sit at our table, waiting for supper when, horrors! The galley door is stuck and the keys have been forgotten, so the guard comes to force his way in. When he broke into the galley, we all cheered! A hot meal, and excellent it was too ... a lovely steak. And of course, we all end up being psychoanalysed. I find I am a very troubled person! Oh dear! But a great journey, entertaining and one of the best because we arrive on time ...

Friday, March 3, 1989.
Flew up to Newcastle. Man tries to engage me in conversation on the plane. What do I do? Oh, TV? ... Do I ever wish I could do the in front of camera presenting ... ? I smile and say, 'Oh, no — I'm much too shy to do that ... '

I am still hurting from an article in a national newspaper about a mistake I made on air when I mixed up my Coca Colas with my Pepsi's ...

Sunday, March 12, 1989.
18.34 Carlisle to London.
Horrid journey. Engineering works on the line. Should have been in at 22.50. Arrive at 00.45. Routed round the Settle line, which would have been glorious to see if only it hadn't been pitch-dark. Get some welcome tea and biscuits from the lovely catering crew ...

Wednesday, March 22, 1989.
07.44 Carlisle to London.
Been on the train five minutes and the guard is still talking ... 'This is the train to London , calling at x, y and z and all points north, east south and west of the compass ... and the luggage has to go overhead, not in the aisles, and please do not get on the train if you are not travelling ... please get off, please close the doors, please do not smoke where you shouldn't ...' Heavens! Man opposite me starts to whistle. After ten minutes, I glare at him, but he doesn't take the hint, so I move down the carriage. At each stop the preamble is the same ... 'Do not enter if you are not travelling, please ensure the luggage ... this is the train calling at x, y and z, but not at p, q and r'. Now his announcements are getting longer and he's starting to tell us not only which station we're coming to, but also which platform! I suppose I shouldn't be awful ... it is quite useful ... but not when you're trying to sleep ...

Sunday, March 26th, 1989.
I brave the sleeper from London to Carlisle.
What a night! Rattle, rattle all the way. Part of the problem is the door, so I try to wedge my makeup between the handle and the lock. Needless to say, it keeps falling down and the rattling continues. Rechristen it 'the Waker'. Nice steward brings welcome tea in the morning and also helps me find a trolley for my many bags and my sewing machine. A sewing machine?! Yes, I never travel without it, it's most useful for running up a few curtains in the carriages ... Actually, I've just bought it in London and am taking it home ...

Monday, April 3, 1989.
Read today that BR are to bring back toast on the trains! Hurray!

Tuesday, April 4, 1989.

Travel home and sit in restaurant car. Couple near me complain when a plastic tray, set for dinner, arrives for each of them. Why no tablecloth, they ask? 'Oh', says the steward, 'it's not like the old days. A lot of people are leaving the service because they don't like to give people plastic things to eat off'. 'Just wait', says the man, 'I'll complain to BR.'

'Just wait till you're halfway up Shap Fell', says the steward cheerfully, 'the tray will probably end up in your lap!' He leaves, but returns with a tablecloth ten minutes later for the disgruntled couple. 'I'll probably get shot for doing this', he says with a wink, '... not sticking to procedure.' Full marks for initiative that chap!

The Glasgow guard gets on at Preston and he's a real character. He brings a few elderly folk to sit in first class because of the overcrowding, singing as he does so. Then at Oxenholme, he comes up to me ... 'Did you leave something in the toilet, madam?', he asks loudly. I go bright red ... what did I leave? He then produces my wallet filled with all my credit cards ...

Monday, May 15, 1989.
New timetable and there seems to be more trains! Good!

Wednesday, June 7, 1989.
Flew home. Late. Will take the train in future ...

Friday, June 9, 1989.
Back to London on train. Really good and we do it in 3 hours 40, our best so far ... is BR looking up?

Wednesday, June 28, 1989.
Rail strike.

Friday, July 14, 1989.
16.52 Carlisle to London.
Now this is how I remember BR! When the train gets to Carlisle, it has been on the go for several hours and is littered with rubbish. I get into first class but it is shabby and dirty. Resolve to complain. Put my hand down side of seat and find one half of a pair of false teeth ... yuk! Move straightaway ...

Tuesday, July 18, 1989.
Rail strike.

123

Tuesday, Aug 22, 1989.
Back to London on the 18.28. Should have got an earlier train, but was fishing ... didn't catch anything though.

Friday, Aug 25, 1989
What a terrible journey! Rushed from the studio to get the 18.30 to Carlisle. Carriage is appalling. Cigarette ash all over seats, curtains hanging off, lots of noise and drunken people around. Complain to guard who says, 'You should have got on the other train, it was even worse ... ' Go to buffet at Crewe and find nothing at all to eat. But, on the bright side, a man near me takes a bottle of champagne from his briefcase and asks if I'd like to share it. It seems quite safe with lots of other folk around, so we drink it and because we haven't eaten, we get a little merry ... Husband not happy at the other end, 'You've been drinking with strange men ... '

Tuesday, September 5, 1989.
18.28 Carlisle to London.
Went first class and spent the time debating whether to give up work at ITN and become a Borders' housewife. What a few weeks of horrid travel and a week's great fishing on the Border Esk can do to a girl! I'll be OK once I'm at Euston, I know it. The guard is now squinting at me ... yes, he's knows who I am ... 'You're that Carol Barnes!'

Friday, September 22, 1989.
Go up north on the evening train with a Russian chap ... as one does. He produces a small tin of caviar, as Russians do, and we go to the restaurant car and ask if we can have some toast and butter. They look dubious, but secret words and whatever else change hands and the toast and butter magically appear along with a bottle of champagne. Is this how Russian men treat their women?! I doubt if I will ever again sit eating caviar and drinking champagne as I speed along the Lake District hills with the sun going down. It must surely be the only way to travel ...

Thursday, October 5, 1989
Will never complain about the trains again! Try to fly to Glasgow, but miss flight due to huge queues at security. Get on next one, two hours later. Taxi out to runway and I have never seen anything like it — thirty or so planes, all waiting to take off before us ...! I eventually get home hours late. Oh, God, why do we do it?

Index

125